Teach Yourself Origami

Second Revised Edition

Other books by John Montroll:

Dinosaur Origami

Mythological Creatures and the Chinese Zodiac Origami

Origami Worldwide by John Montroll and Brian K. Webb

Origami Under the Sea by John Montroll and Robert J. Lang

Sea Creatures in Origami by John Montroll and Robert J. Lang

Bringing Origami to Life

Bugs and Birds in Origami

Dollar Bill Animals in Origami

Dollar Bill Origami

Easy Dollar Bill Origami

Super Simple Origami

A Constellation of Origami Polyhedra

Classic Polyhedra Origami

Storytime Origami

Christmas Origami

Easy Christmas Origami

Animal Origami for the Enthusiast

Origami for the Enthusiast

Easy Origami

Birds in Origami

Favorite Animals in Origami

Teach Yourself Origami

Second Revised Edition

John Montroll

Dover Publications, Inc.
New York

To Jeremy, Christine, and Gabriel

Library of Congress Cataloging-in-Publication Data

Montroll, John.
  Teach yourself origami / John Montroll. -- Rev. ed.
     p. cm.
  ISBN 978-0-486-48363-4
  1. Origami. I. Title.
  TT870.M574   ISBN-10: 0-486-48363-0   2011
  736'.982--dc22
                        2011011470

              Manufactured in the United States
                        48363001
              www.doverpublications.com

Introduction

elcome to the wonderful and magic world of origami. This collection teaches the new folder how to get started in origami and to systematically aquire more skills. The first part of the book introduces techniques and maneuvers, and builds upon them using simple models as examples. Intermediate and advanced models are gradually added, and students quickly find themselves origami masters.

This book can also be used as a text or lesson plan for individuals, schools or origami courses. Start from the beginning of the book, and fold through it, one model at a time. Diagram symbols, techniques, and terminology are introduced progressively, and each model builds upon the skills aquired in completing prior ones.

Every model has been tested by novices. Nothing included here is impossible, but some areas require practice to perfect. If you find a new technique especially difficult to acquire, persevere. Start again from the beginning, or put the model aside and try again later.

There are many styles of origami, and many approaches. In this book I have included only models which can be folded from one uncut square. Some of the origami in the first chapter are traditional, and two pieces in the advanced chapter were created by Fred Rohm, an American origami pioneer. Any models without credit are my designs.

This work is a revision of my previous title *Teach Yourself Origami*. There are more simple models in chapter 1. Some of the models in chapters 2 and 3 have been revised or replaced.

As in all my books, the illustrations conform to the internationally accepted Randlett-Yoshizawa conventions. These symbols are used in most recently published diagrams, so learning them will open the pages of other origami books, too. The colored side of origami paper is represented by the shadings in the diagrams. Origami supplies can be found in arts and craft shops, or visit Dover Publications online at www.doverpublications.com, or OrigamiUSA at www.origami-usa.org. Large sheets are easier to use than small ones.

Many people helped make this book possible. I wish to thank Beth Maccallum for introducing Fred Rohm's models to me, and Krista Willett for introducing them to Beth. Special thanks to Bea Rohm for her permission to use Fred's models. I would also like to thank Jan Polish for her work as editor. I give special thanks to Himanshu Agrawal for folding the models for the cover. Of course I also thank the many folders who proof-read the diagrams.

John Montroll

www.johnmontroll.com

Contents

★ Simple
★★ Intermediate
★★★ Complex

━━━━━━━━ **Chapter 1: Beginner ★** ━━━━━━━━

Cup
page 12

Samurai Hat
page 13

House
page 14

Pin Wheel
page 15

House
page 17

Piano
page 17

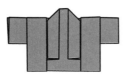
Kimono
page 18

Sailboat
page 20

Candy Dish
page 21

Waterbomb
page 23

Church
page 24

Fortune Teller
page 25

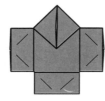
Yakko-San
page 26

Sanbow
page 26

Table
page 29

Box
page 31

Peacock
page 33

Parakeet
page 34

Flapping Bird
page 36

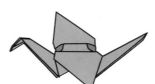
Crane
page 36

Lily
page 38

Frog
page 39

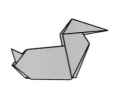
Duck
page 40

Swan
page 41

Penguin
page 41

Fish
page 43

Face
page 43

Star
page 47

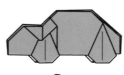
Car
page 50

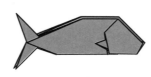
Fish
page 52

Moat Monster
page 54

Chapter 2: Intermediate ★★

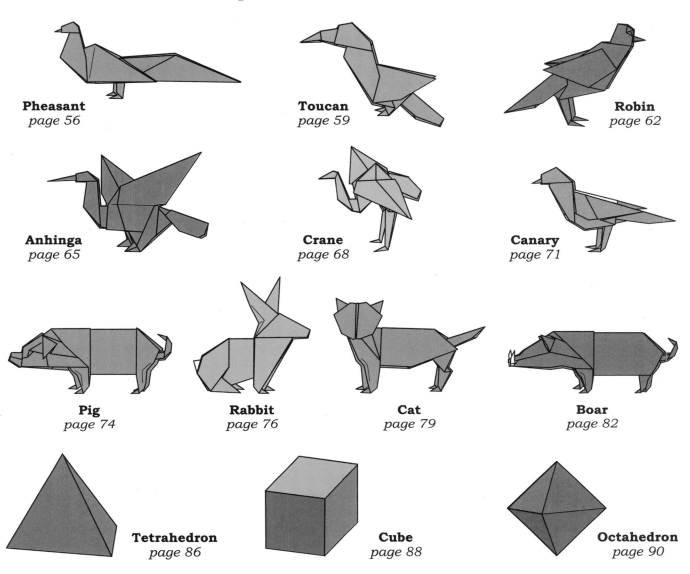

Chapter 3: Advanced ★★★

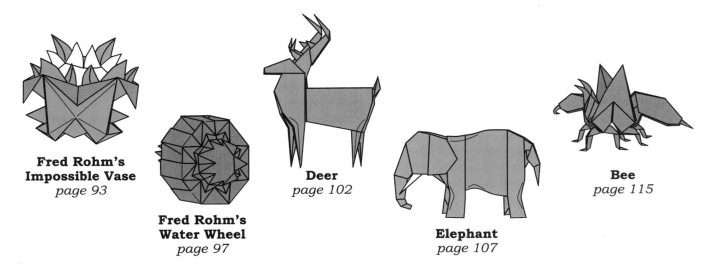

Symbols

Lines

— — — — — — — — — — Valley fold, fold in front.

—·—·—··—·—··—··— — Mountain fold, fold behind.

———————————— Crease line.

··· X-ray or guide line.

Arrows

Fold in this direction.

Fold behind.

Unfold.

Fold and unfold.

Turn over.

Sink or three dimensional folding.

Place your finger between these layers.

Chapter 1—Beginner

Getting Started

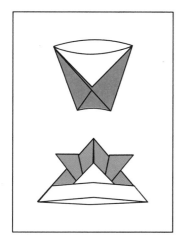

Pull Out

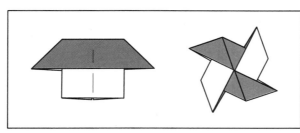

Squash Fold

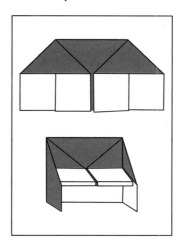

Someone who has not folded can learn the basics from this chapter. New techniques are shown one at a time, along with several traditional Japanese models. There are even a few practice models.

When you fold something for the first time it could seem difficult. If you do have trouble, fold very slowly and carefully and do not give up. Once you have managed something new, fold it again to see how much easier it becomes.

Preliminary Fold

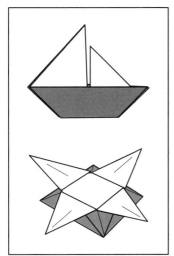

Waterbomb Base

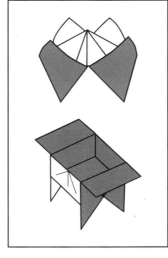

Blintz Fold

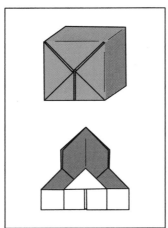

Petal Fold

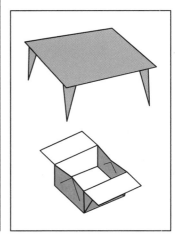

Bird Base

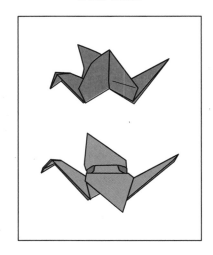

Reverse Fold

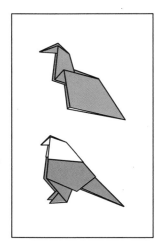

Frog Base

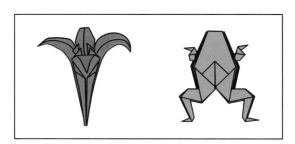

Each model teaches a new maneuver. It would be better not to skip any. After the completion of the chapter you will have folded the waterbomb (balloon), famous crane, frog, and many other traditional favorites along with a few of my own.

Outside Reverse Fold

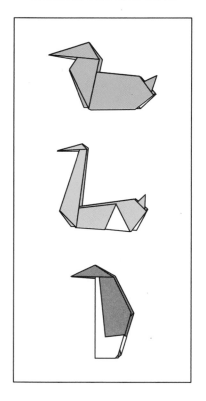

Rabbit Ear

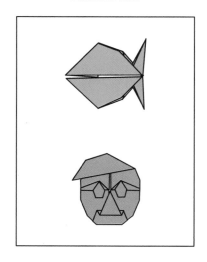

Sink

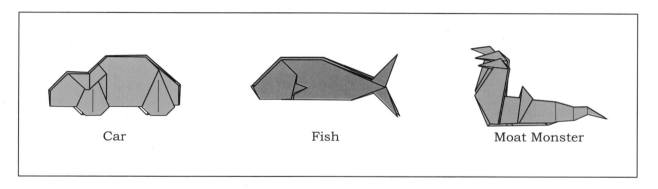

Car   Fish   Moat Monster

Following the diagrams:

1. Origami paper is colored on one side, white on the other. The shading in the diagrams represents the colored side. In the first step of each model, check which side begins face up.

2. In each step, check for the kind of folds being done, along with possible landmarks.

3. Make sure you look at the next step to see the result.

4. Hold your paper exactly as shown in the diagram, note any instructions to turn over or rotate the model.

5. Be sure not to skip steps. It is perhaps the most common mistake.

Structures and Bases

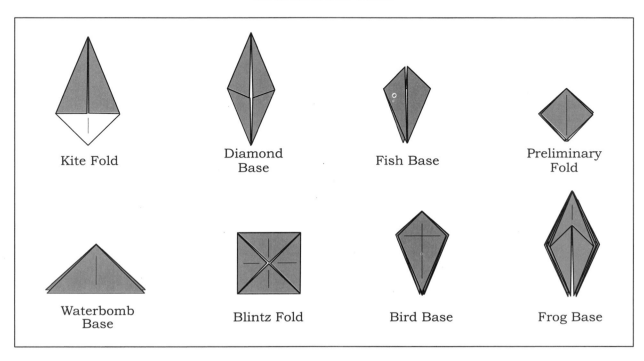

Kite Fold   Diamond Base   Fish Base   Preliminary Fold

Waterbomb Base   Blintz Fold   Bird Base   Frog Base

Getting Started

Cup *Traditional*

For the first model, all of the new symbols
are used. Every step uses landmarks so each
fold is given an exact location. It is fun to
fold a model a few times and memorize it;
this helps the folding to become automatic.

1

Begin with the
white side face up,
fold in half, corner
to corner.

2

Though the corners at the top
should meet, they are
separated in the diagram for
clarity. Fold one side down.

3

Unfold.

4

Fold the corner to the dot.

5

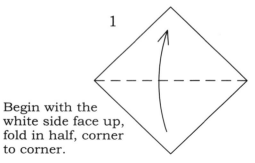

Fold the other corner.

6

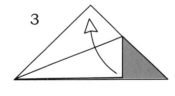

Fold one layer down.

7

Fold behind along
the mountain fold
line.

8

Place your
finger inside to
open the cup.

9

Cup

Samurai Hat Traditional

For this model, a few folds are done without landmarks. This means that you can change the angle or position of these folds so that each hat will be different.

New Symbol:

Turn over.

1

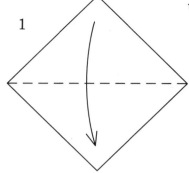

Begin with the white side up. Fold in half.

2

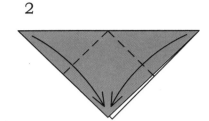

Fold the corners down, one at a time, to meet at the bottom.

3

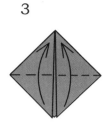

Fold the corners up, one at a time.

4

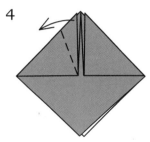

Fold a corner so it sticks out. There is no landmark.

5

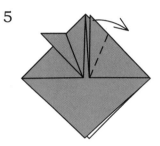

Repeat on the other side.

6

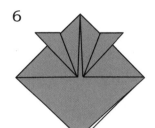

Turn over.

7

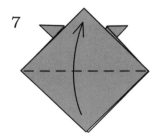

Fold one layer up.

8

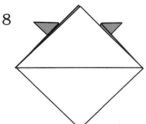

9

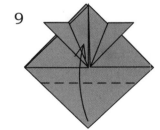

Fold up. There are no landmarks.

10

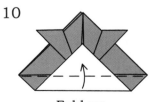

Fold up.

11

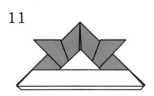

Place your finger inside to open the hat.

12

Samurai Hat

Pull Out

The concept of pulling out comes in many forms. Sometimes the results can be surprising. Look carefully at the direction of the arrow and at the next step.

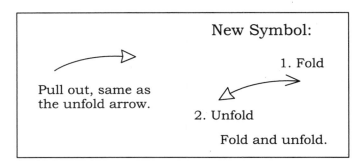
House Traditional

This simple model gives an example of pulling out a corner. It begins with pre-creasing.

1
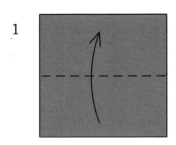

Fold up.

2

Unfold.

3
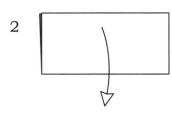

Fold in half and unfold.

4
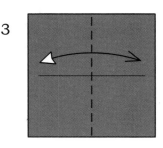

Fold up to the center crease.

5
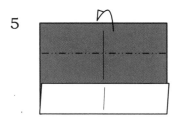

Mountain-fold (fold behind) to the center crease.

6

Fold to the center.

7
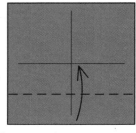

Pull out the top layer, follow the dot in steps 7–9.

8
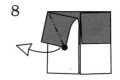

Here is a 3D intermediate view.

9

Pull out.

10
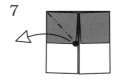

Turn over.

11
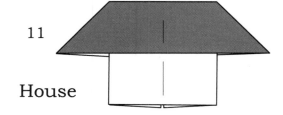

House

Pin Wheel Traditional

For this example all four corners will be pulled out. Like the house, it begins with pre-creasing.

New Symbol:

 This arrow shows between which layers of paper to place your finger.

1

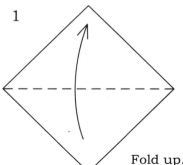

Fold up.

2

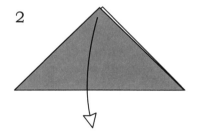

Unfold.

3

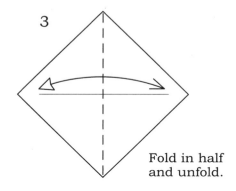

Fold in half and unfold.

4

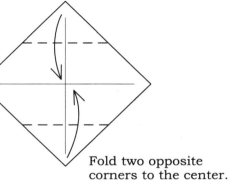

Fold two opposite corners to the center.

5

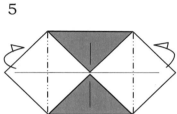

Fold the corners behind.

6

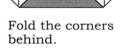

Fold two corners to the center.

7

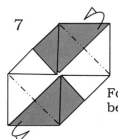

Fold the corners behind.

8

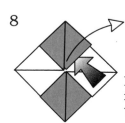

Place your finger inside to pull out the corner.

9

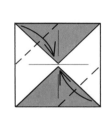

Pull out the lower corner.

10

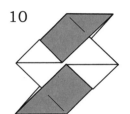

11

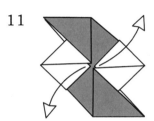

Pull out the white corners.

12

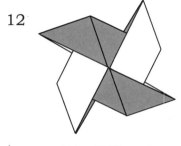

Pin Wheel

Squash Fold

In a squash fold, some paper is opened and then made flat. The shaded arrow shows where to place your finger.

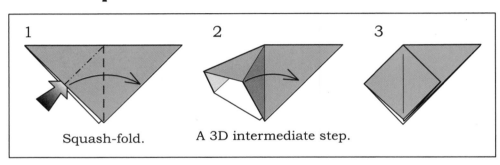

1

2   A 3D intermediate step.

3

Squash-fold.

Many Squash Folds Practice Model

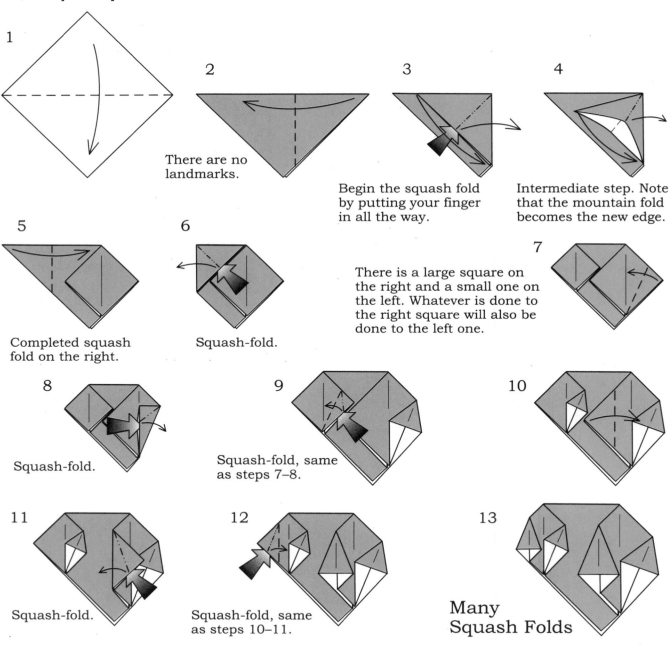

1

2   There are no landmarks.

3   Begin the squash fold by putting your finger in all the way.

4   Intermediate step. Note that the mountain fold becomes the new edge.

5   Completed squash fold on the right.

6   Squash-fold.

There is a large square on the right and a small one on the left. Whatever is done to the right square will also be done to the left one.

7

8   Squash-fold.

9   Squash-fold, same as steps 7–8.

10

11   Squash-fold.

12   Squash-fold, same as steps 10–11.

13   Many Squash Folds

House Traditional

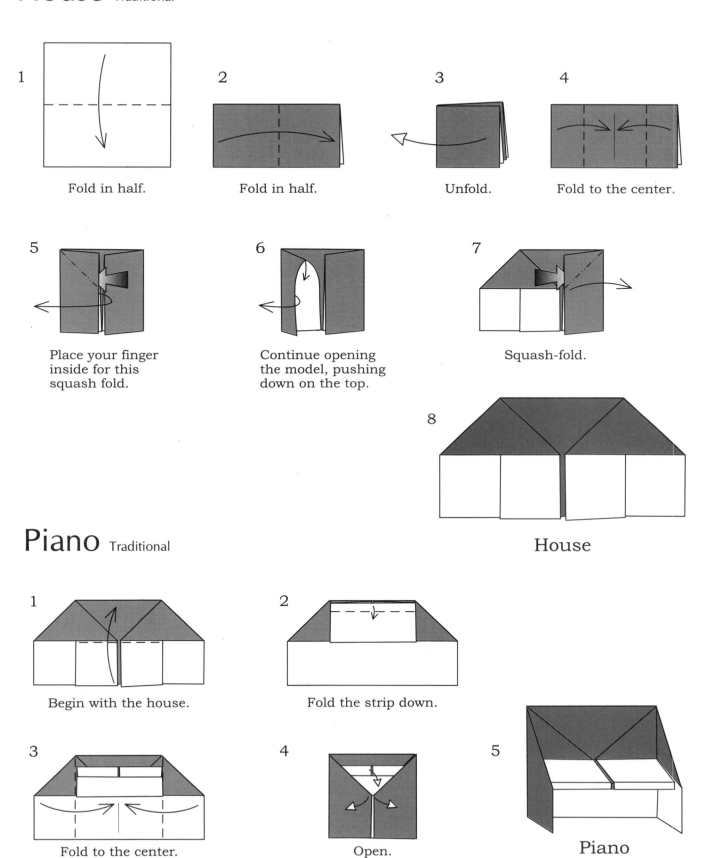

1 Fold in half.

2 Fold in half.

3 Unfold.

4 Fold to the center.

5 Place your finger inside for this squash fold.

6 Continue opening the model, pushing down on the top.

7 Squash-fold.

8 House

Piano Traditional

1 Begin with the house.

2 Fold the strip down.

3 Fold to the center.

4 Open.

5 Piano

Kimono Traditional

In many models, some steps are repeated. For clarity in the folding procedure, and to save steps while diagramming, it is common to mention which steps are repeated. For this kimono, step 11 says "Repeat steps 9–10 on the right."

1

Fold in half.

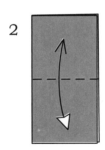

2

Fold and unfold.

3

Fold a thin strip.

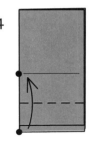

4

Fold the bottom to the crease.

5

Fold towards the center and bottom.

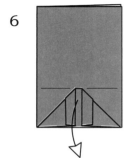

6

Unfold.

7

Fold up so the dot is slightly above the crease.

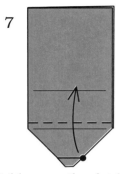

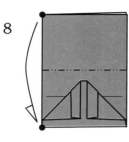

8

Fold in half.

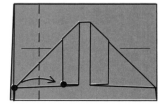

9

The dots will meet.

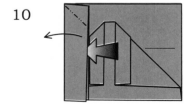

10

Squash-fold.

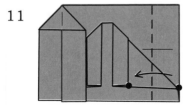

11

Repeat steps 9–10 on the right.

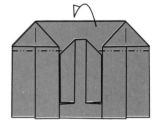

12

Fold behind.

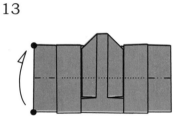

13

Fold behind.

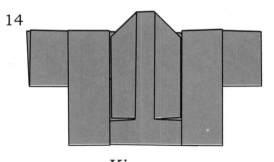

14

Kimono

Preliminary Fold

The preliminary fold is the beginning shape of thousands of origami designs. It is named because two bases, the bird base and frog base, are folded from it. Two folding methods are given, though method 2 provides the preliminary fold in a more accurate manner. If you fold the preliminary folds using each method, you will be ready to begin the next two models. Throughout the book, the preliminary fold will be diagrammed as shown to the right.

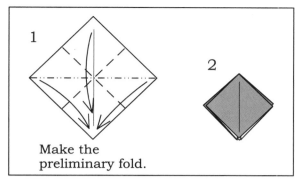

Make the preliminary fold.

Method 1—Uses squash folds.

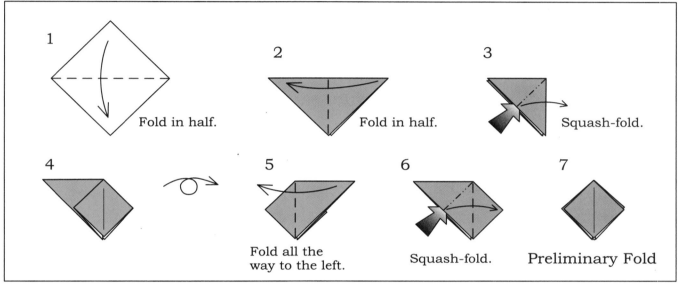

1 Fold in half.

2 Fold in half.

3 Squash-fold.

4

5 Fold all the way to the left.

6 Squash-fold.

7 Preliminary Fold

Method 2—Uses fold and unfold.

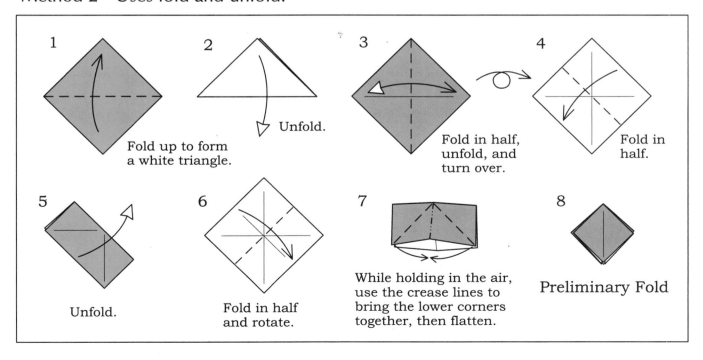

1 Fold up to form a white triangle.

2 Unfold.

3 Fold in half, unfold, and turn over.

4 Fold in half.

5 Unfold.

6 Fold in half and rotate.

7 While holding in the air, use the crease lines to bring the lower corners together, then flatten.

8 Preliminary Fold

Sailboat Traditional

This sailboat is the logo for *OrigamiUSA*. Note the jagged arrow in step 11. This indicates the different directions the paper will go.

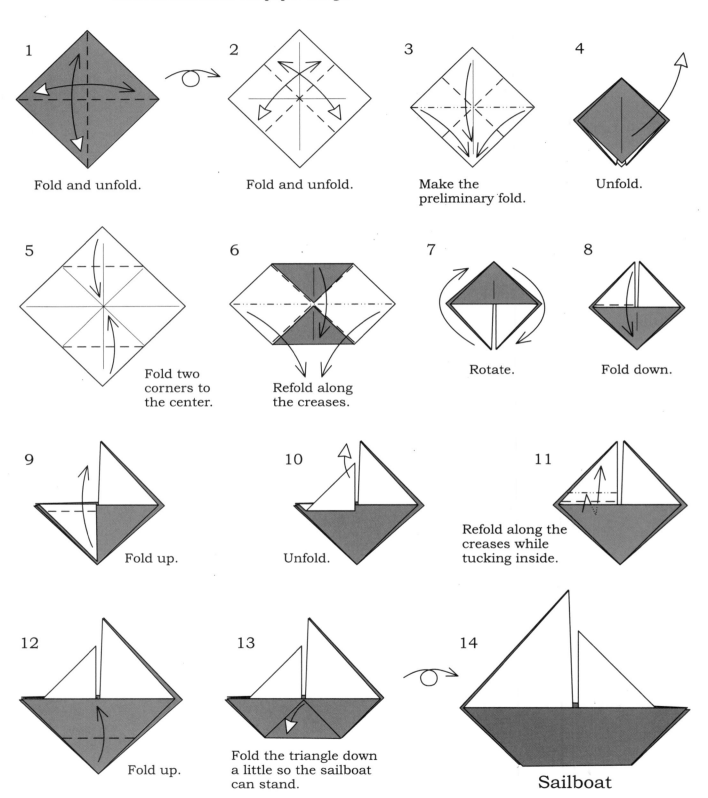

1 Fold and unfold.

2 Fold and unfold.

3 Make the preliminary fold.

4 Unfold.

5 Fold two corners to the center.

6 Refold along the creases.

7 Rotate.

8 Fold down.

9 Fold up.

10 Unfold.

11 Refold along the creases while tucking inside.

12 Fold up.

13 Fold the triangle down a little so the sailboat can stand.

14 Sailboat

Candy Dish Traditional

This model introduces a maneuver called the minor miracle (step 10). This fold is like turning pages of a book.

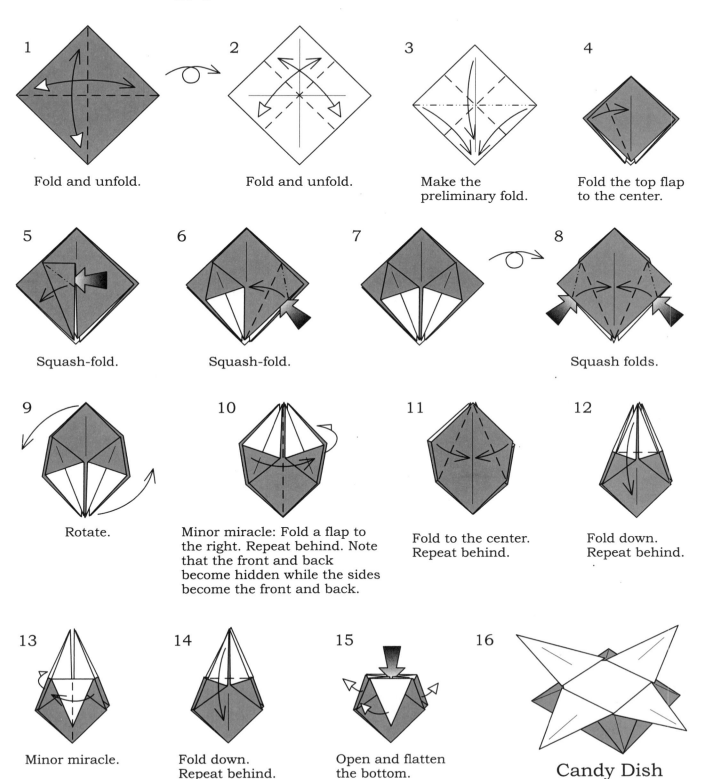

1 Fold and unfold.

2 Fold and unfold.

3 Make the preliminary fold.

4 Fold the top flap to the center.

5 Squash-fold.

6 Squash-fold.

7

8 Squash folds.

9 Rotate.

10 Minor miracle: Fold a flap to the right. Repeat behind. Note that the front and back become hidden while the sides become the front and back.

11 Fold to the center. Repeat behind.

12 Fold down. Repeat behind.

13 Minor miracle.

14 Fold down. Repeat behind.

15 Open and flatten the bottom.

16 Candy Dish

Waterbomb Base

The waterbomb base is named from the waterbomb balloon which is made from it. Throughout the book the waterbomb base will be diagrammed as shown to the right.

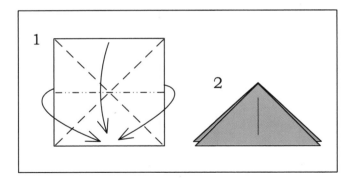

Waterbomb Base

1
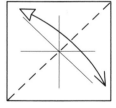
Fold up and unfold.

2
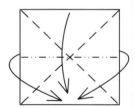
Fold and unfold.

3
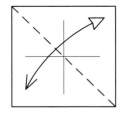
Fold and unfold.

4
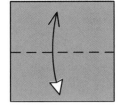
Fold and unfold.

5
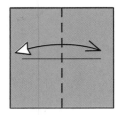
Collapse along the creases.

6
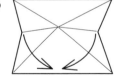
A 3D intermediate step.

7
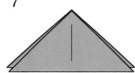
Waterbomb Base

The waterbomb base and preliminary fold are inside-out versions of each other. Each can easily be folded into the other with reversed colors.

1
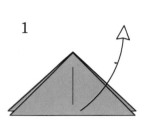
Begin with the waterbomb base. Unfold.

2
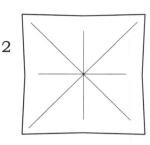
Rotate.

3
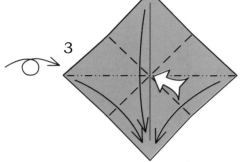
Push in the center and fold along the creases.

4

Preliminary Fold

Waterbomb Traditional

1

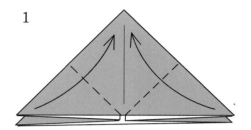

Begin with the waterbomb base. Fold the corners up. Repeat behind.

2

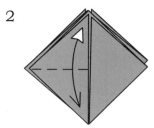

Fold one layer down and unfold.

3

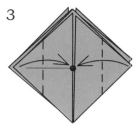

Fold to the center. Repeat behind.

4

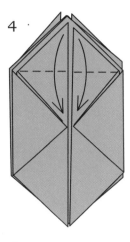

Fold to the center. Repeat behind.

5

Fold along the edge of the top layers. Repeat behind.

6

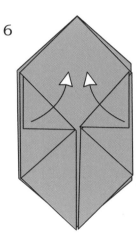

Unfold. Repeat behind.

7

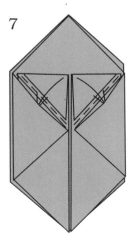

Tuck inside the pockets. Repeat behind.

8

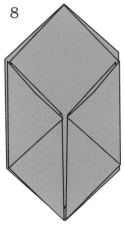

Holding the model like a star, with your fingers between the layers, blow into the bottom.

9

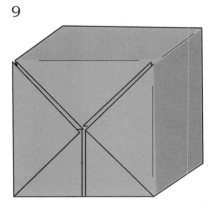

Waterbomb

Church _{Traditional}

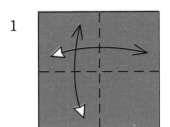

1

Fold and unfold.

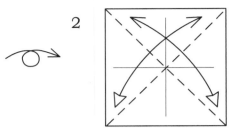

2

Fold and unfold.

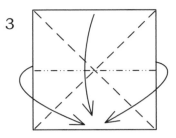

3

Collapse along
the creases.

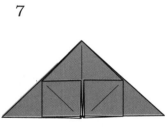

4

This is the
Waterbomb Base.
Fold the flap up.

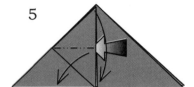

5

Squash-fold.

6

Repeat steps 4–5
on the right.

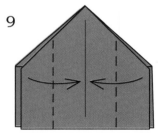

7

Repeat steps
4–6 behind.

8

Fold to the right and
repeat behind. This is
a minor miracle.

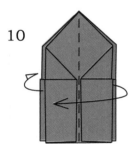

9

Fold the top layers
to the center.
Repeat behind.

10

Minor miracle.

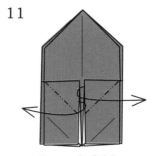

11

Squash folds.

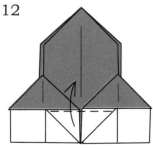

12

Fold up.

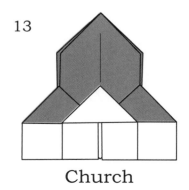

13

Church

Blintz Fold

In a blintz fold, the four corners are folded to the center to make a smaller square with more points. Using the additional points, more points are then available to fold. Many things folded from a square can be folded from the blintz fold.

Blintz Fold

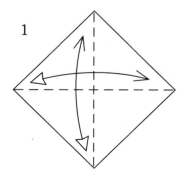

1

Fold and unfold.

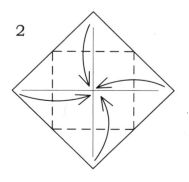

2

Fold the corners to the center.

3

Blintz Fold

Fortune Teller Traditional

1

Begin with the blintz fold.

2

Blintz again.

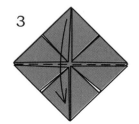

3

Fold in half.

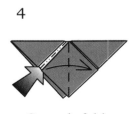

4

Squash-fold.

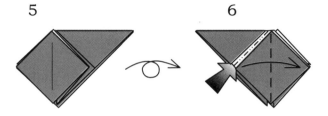

5

6

Squash-fold.

7

Spread the four corners.

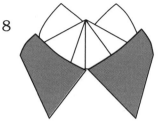

8

Fortune Teller (or Cootie Catcher)

In England this is often used as a salt cellar, and in Japan as a candy dish.

Yakko-San Traditional

1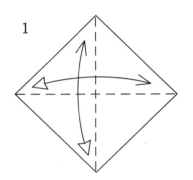

Fold and unfold.

2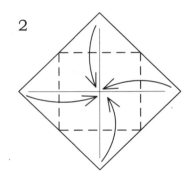

Blintz.

3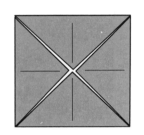

This is the Blintz Fold.

4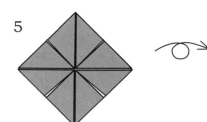

Blintz again.

5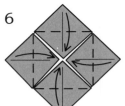

6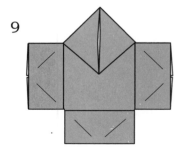

Another blintz.

7

Turn over and rotate.

8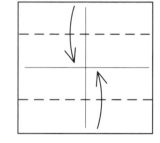

Open on three sides.

9

Yakko-San

Wrestler

Sanbow Traditional

1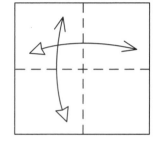

Fold and unfold.

2

Fold to the center.

3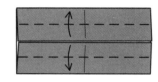

Fold the top layers.

4

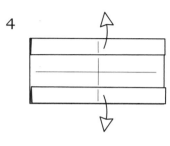

Unfold.

5

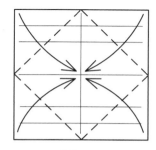

Blintz.

6

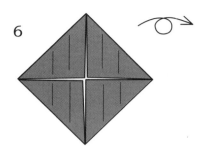

7

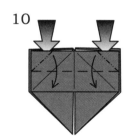

Fold and unfold.

8

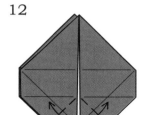

This is the same as
the preliminary fold.

9

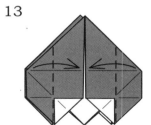

Open while folding
up. Repeat behind.

10

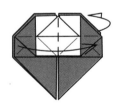

Squash-fold on
the left and right.
Repeat behind.

11

Fold to the right
and repeat behind.
Rotate 180°.

12

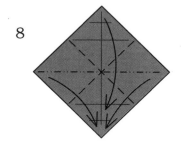

Repeat behind.

13

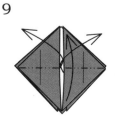

Fold to the center.
Repeat behind.

14

Fold down.
Repeat behind.

15

Fold down.
Repeat behind.

16

Spread the box.

17

Sanbow

Petal Fold

In a petal fold, one point is folded up while two opposite sides meet each other.

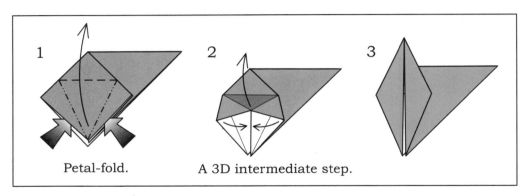

1

2

3

Petal-fold.   A 3D intermediate step.

Two Petal Folds Practice Model

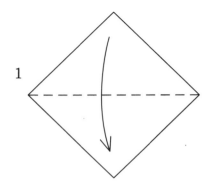

1

2

3

Squash-fold.

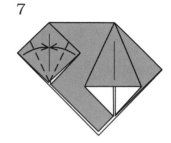

4

Completed squash fold on the right.

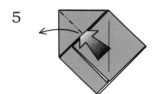

5

Squash-fold.

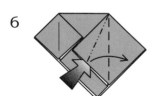

6

Squash-fold.

7

Fold to the center.

8

Unfold.

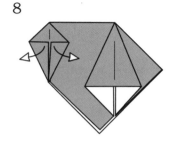

9

At the moment there is no line between the dots. Imagine that line, shown as a dotted line. Begin by folding on it and the rest of the folds will fall into place.

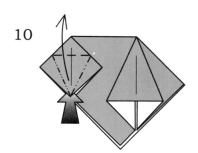

10

Lift the top layer up, forming a new fold only on that imaginary line, now shown as a valley fold. You will be changing the direction of the two other folds in the top layer, but not forming any folds that are not already in the paper. The completed petal fold is shown in step 13.

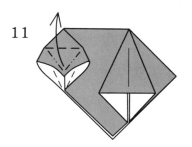

11

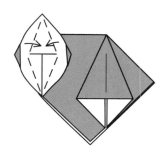

12

Intermediate steps. This petal fold will form a diamond as seen on the left in step 13.

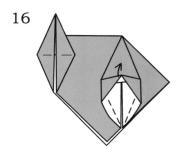

13

Fold to the center.

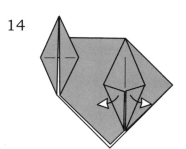

14

Unfold.

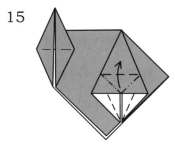

15

Petal-fold. Begin by folding only on the imaginary line shown as a valley fold line.

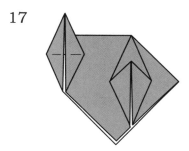

16

Intermediate step.

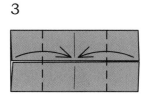

17

Two Petal Folds

Table Traditional

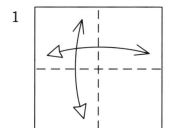

1

Fold and unfold.

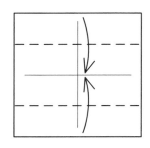

2

Fold to the center.

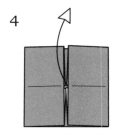

3

Fold to the center.

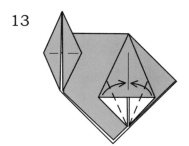

4

Pull out.

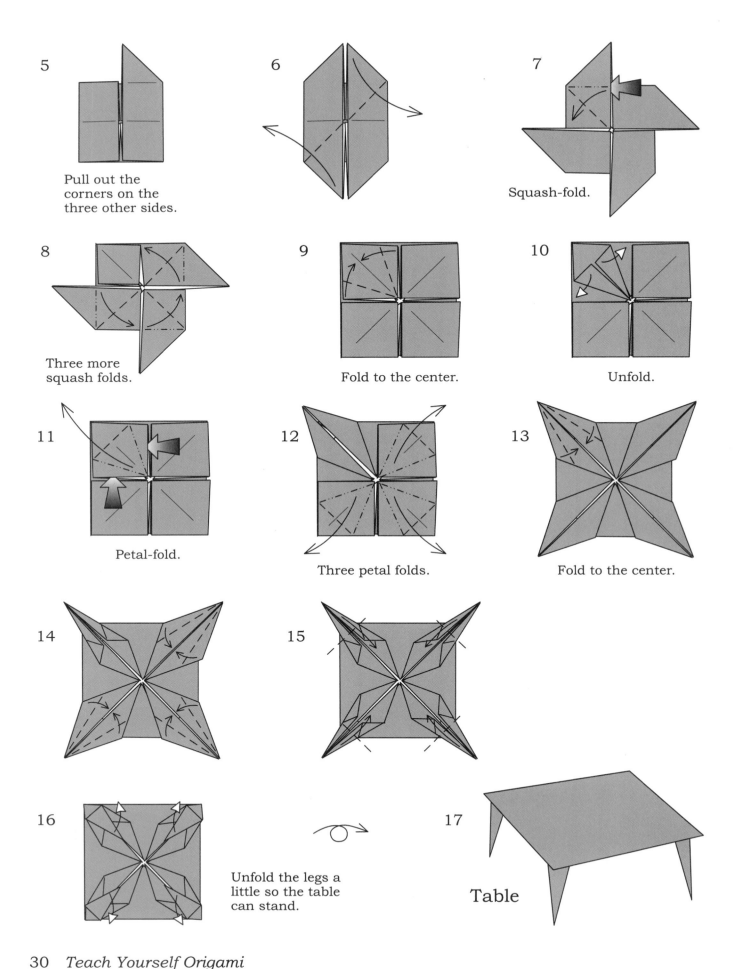

5

Pull out the
corners on the
three other sides.

6

7

Squash-fold.

8

Three more
squash folds.

9

Fold to the center.

10

Unfold.

11

Petal-fold.

12

Three petal folds.

13

Fold to the center.

14

15

16

Unfold the legs a
little so the table
can stand.

17

Table

Box Traditional

Another form of the petal
fold is used for the box.

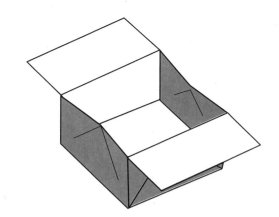

1

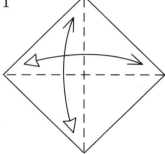

Fold and unfold.

2

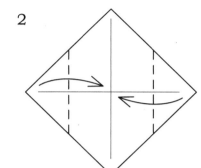

Fold two opposite
corners to the center.

3

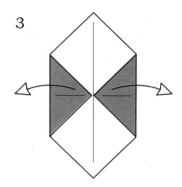

Unfold.

4

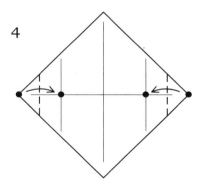

The dots will meet.

5

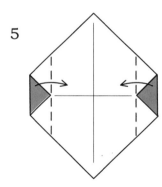

Fold along the creases.

6

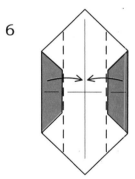

Fold to the center.

7

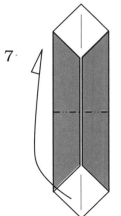

Fold in half.

8

Fold all the layers
to the center.

9

Unfold.

10

This is the start of the petal fold. Open the model so it will be 3D. Bring the edge to the dot. Repeat on the right.

11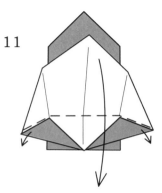

This 3D step shows the petal fold in progress. Flatten.

12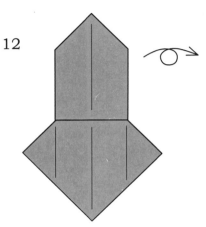

13

14

Unfold.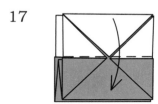

15

Petal-fold.

16

Fold to the center and repeat behind. Rotate the top to the bottom.

17

Repeat behind.

18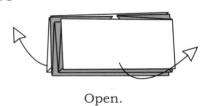

Open.

19

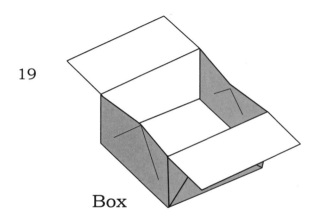

Box

Inside Reverse Fold

In an inside reverse fold, some paper is folded between layers. Here are two examples.

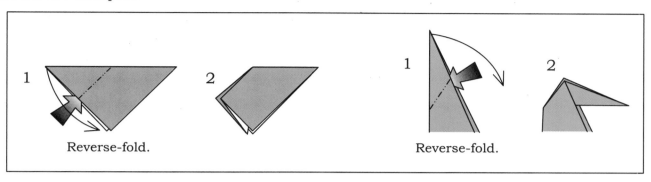

1

Reverse-fold.

2

1

Reverse-fold.

2

Two Reverse Folds Practice Model

There is also an outside reverse fold, to be shown later. The inside reverse fold is much more common, however, and is often called a reverse fold. The kite fold is also introduced.

1

Fold and unfold.

2

Fold to the center.

3

This is the kite fold.

4

Place your finger inside and push the top of the model in the direction of the arrow. The completed fold is shown in step 6.

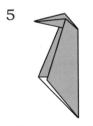

5

A 3D intermediate step.

6

Reverse-fold the bottom inside.

7

Practice Model

Peacock Traditional

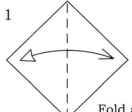

1

Fold and unfold.

2

Kite-fold.

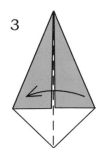

3

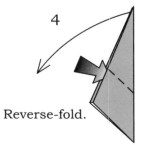

4

Reverse-fold.

5

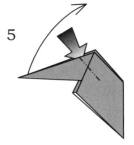

Reverse-fold.

6

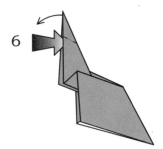

Reverse-fold.

7

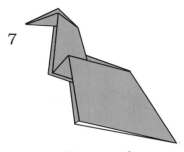

Peacock

Parakeet Traditional

1

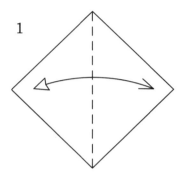

Fold and unfold.

2

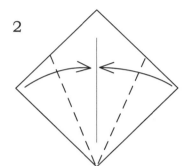

Kite-fold.

3

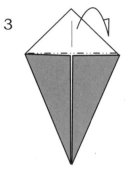

Fold behind.

4

Fold to the center.

5

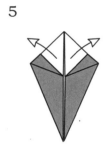

Unfold.

6

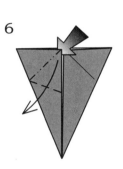

Squash-fold.

7

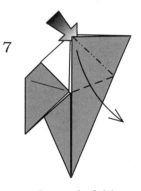

Squash-fold.

8

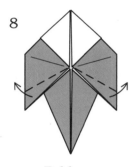

Fold up.

9

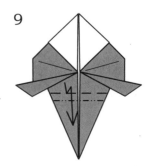

Fold back
and forth.

10

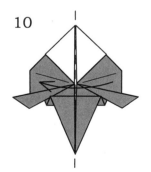

Fold in half
and rotate.

11

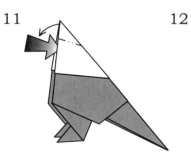

Reverse-fold
the beak.

12

Parakeet

Bird Base

The bird base is possibly the most popular starting point in origami. It is used in thousands of designs. Two of the best known models that begin with the bird base are the flapping bird and crane.

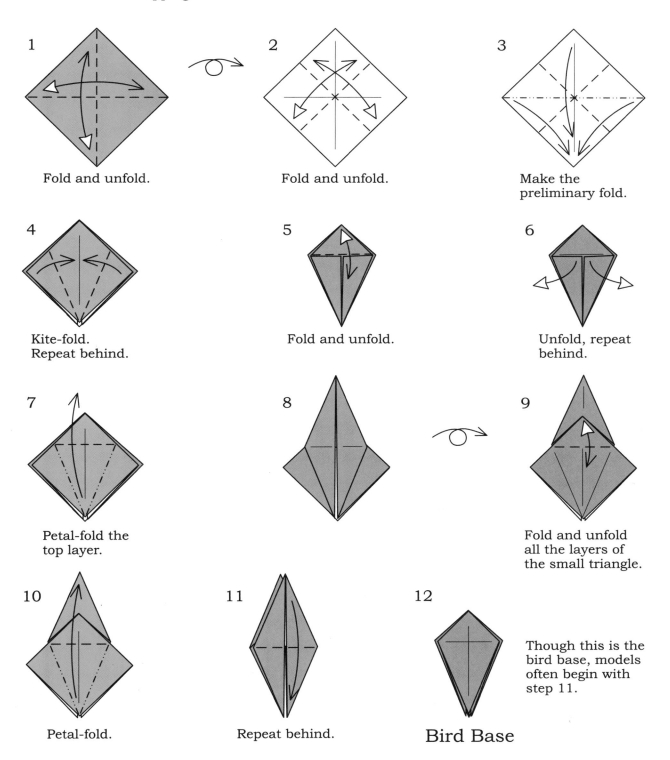

1

Fold and unfold.

2

Fold and unfold.

3

Make the preliminary fold.

4

Kite-fold. Repeat behind.

5

Fold and unfold.

6

Unfold, repeat behind.

7

Petal-fold the top layer.

8

9

Fold and unfold all the layers of the small triangle.

10

Petal-fold.

11

Repeat behind.

12

Though this is the bird base, models often begin with step 11.

Bird Base

Flapping Bird Traditional

1

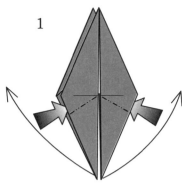

Begin with step 11 of the bird base. Reverse folds.

2

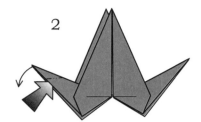

Reverse-fold.

3

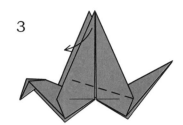

Fold the wing out. Repeat behind.

Pull the tail back and forth while holding at the bottom of the neck. The wings will flap. The white circles show where to hold.

4

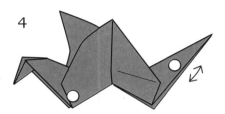

Flapping Bird

Crane Traditional

1

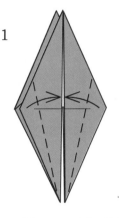

Begin with step 11 of the bird base. For this kite fold, fold close to the center line but not exactly on it. Repeat behind.

2

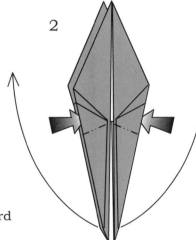

Reverse folds.

3

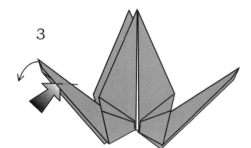

Reverse-fold.

4

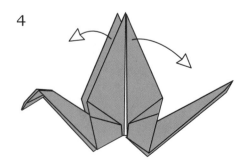

Pull the wings apart and let the body open.

5

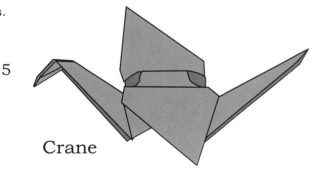

Crane

This is perhaps the most famous model in all of origami. The crane symbolizes peace and hope; a thousand cranes, often strung together, are folded for many occasions. Many Japanese children know this model. Being able to fold it is a milestone.

Frog Base

The frog base is named for the jumping frog folded from it. It starts from the preliminary fold.

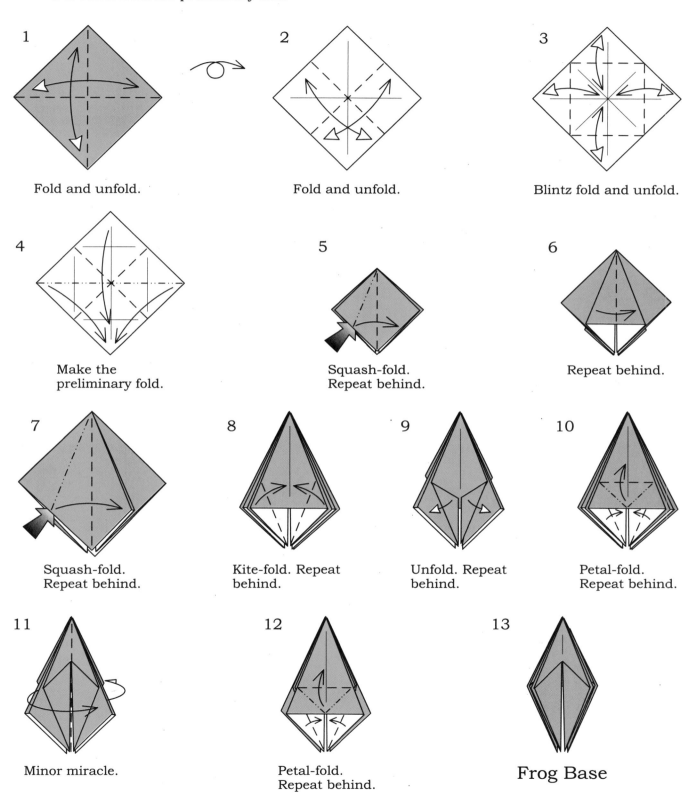

1

Fold and unfold.

2

Fold and unfold.

3

Blintz fold and unfold.

4

Make the
preliminary fold.

5

Squash-fold.
Repeat behind.

6

Repeat behind.

7

Squash-fold.
Repeat behind.

8

Kite-fold. Repeat
behind.

9

Unfold. Repeat
behind.

10

Petal-fold.
Repeat behind.

11

Minor miracle.

12

Petal-fold.
Repeat behind.

13

Frog Base

Lily Traditional

This traditional model makes for a beautiful three dimensional flower.

1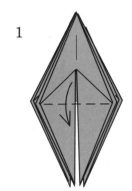

Begin with the frog base. Fold the loose flap down. Repeat behind.

2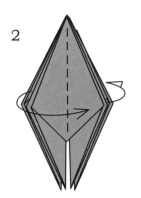

Fold two layers. Repeat behind.

3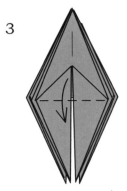

Repeat behind.

4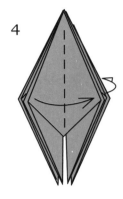

Fold one layer. Repeat behind.

5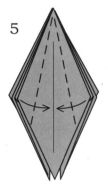

Kite-fold. Repeat behind.

6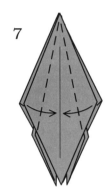

Minor miracle.

7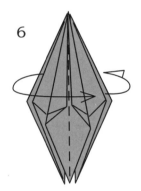

Kite-fold. Repeat behind.

8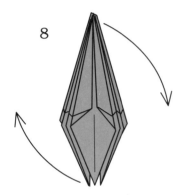

Rotate.

9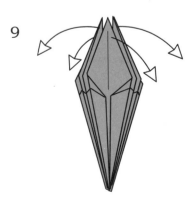

Separate and curl the petals.

10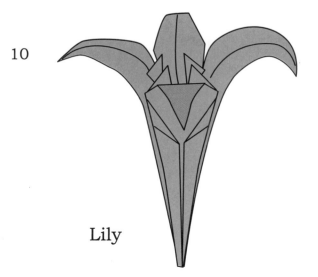

Lily

Frog Traditional

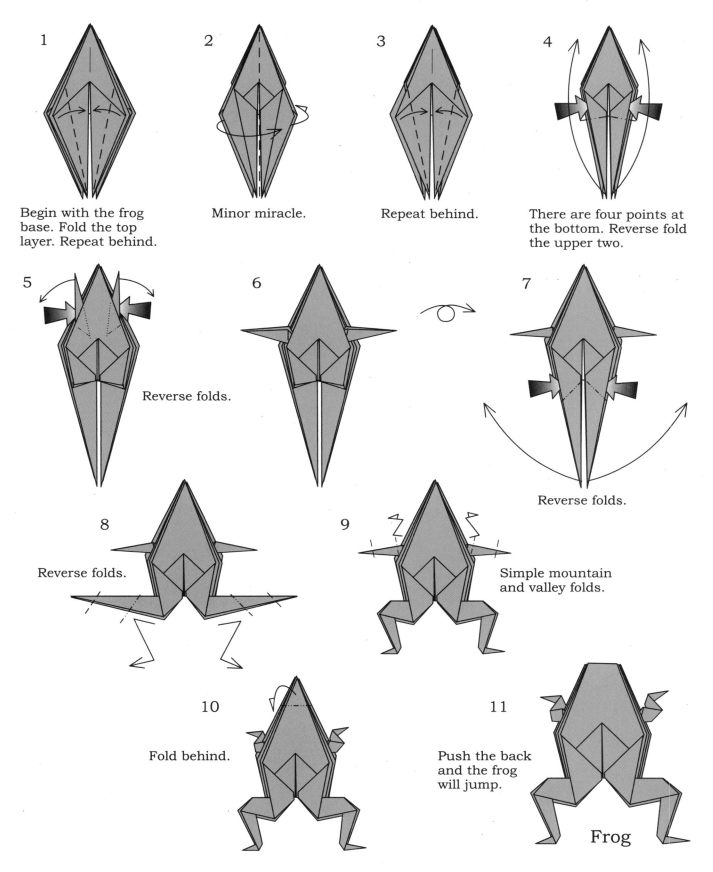

1

Begin with the frog base. Fold the top layer. Repeat behind.

2

Minor miracle.

3

Repeat behind.

4

There are four points at the bottom. Reverse fold the upper two.

5

Reverse folds.

6

7

Reverse folds.

8

Reverse folds.

9

Simple mountain and valley folds.

10

Fold behind.

11

Push the back and the frog will jump.

Frog

Outside Reverse Fold

For an outside reverse fold, the paper will wrap around itself. Much of the paper must be unfolded.

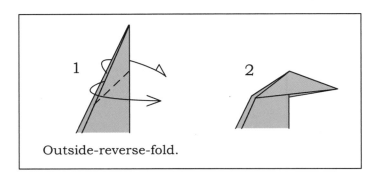

Outside-reverse-fold.

Duck

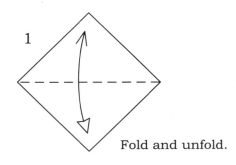

1

Fold and unfold.

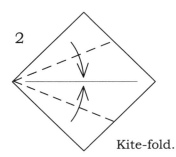

2

Kite-fold.

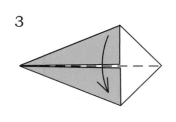

3

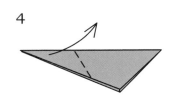

4

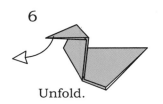

5

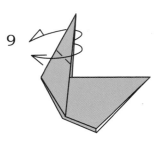

6

Unfold.

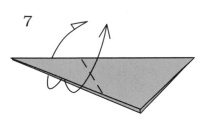

7

Outside-reverse-fold along the crease. Begin by unfolding and wrapping the paper around. Step 9 shows the completed fold.

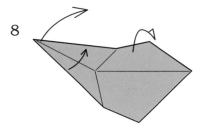

8

This 3D intermediate step shows how the left side wraps around.

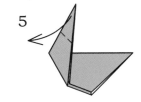

9

Outside-reverse-fold.

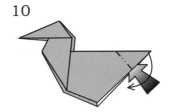

10

Reverse-fold.

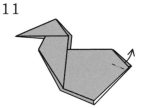

11

Reverse-fold.

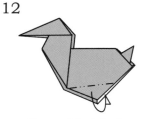

12

Repeat behind.

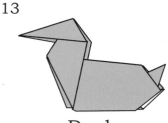

13

Duck

Swan Traditional

1
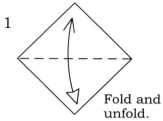
Fold and unfold.

2
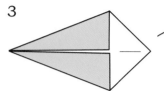
Kite-fold.

3
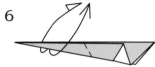

4
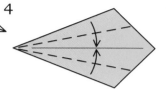

5
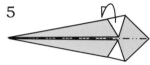
Fold in half or see below for the simple method that avoids the outside reverse folds.

6

Outside-reverse-fold.

7

Outside-reverse-fold.

8
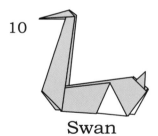
Reverse-fold.

9

Reverse-fold.

10

Swan

Simple Method

5
Begin with step 5 above.

6
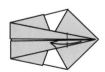

7
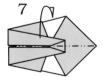
Fold in half.

8
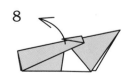
Slide the neck up.

9

Slide the head up. Continue with step 8 above.

Penguin

1
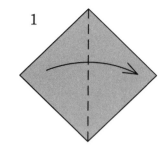

2
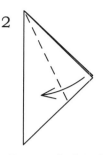
Repeat behind.

3
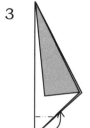
Reverse-fold.

4
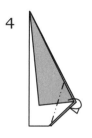
Repeat behind.

5
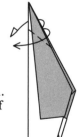
Outside-reverse-fold. See how the angle of the head affects the penguin.

6
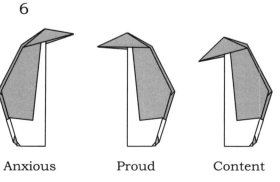
Anxious   Proud   Content
Penguins

Rabbit-Ear

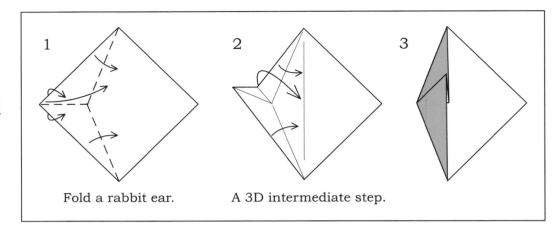

To fold a rabbit ear, one corner is folded in half and laid down to a side.

1

2

3

Fold a rabbit ear.

A 3D intermediate step.

Fish Base

The fish base is made from two rabbit ears.

1

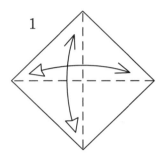

Fold and unfold.

2

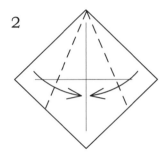

Kite-fold.

3

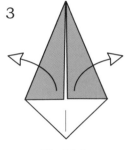

Unfold.

4

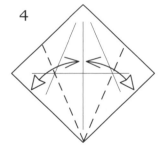

Fold and unfold.

5

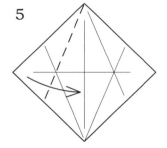

Fold along the crease.

6

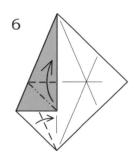

Squash-fold.

7

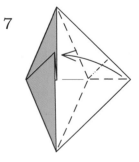

Fold a rabbit ear. The results are the same as on the left.

8

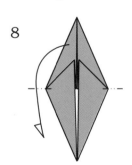

Fold behind.

9

Fish Base

Fish Traditional

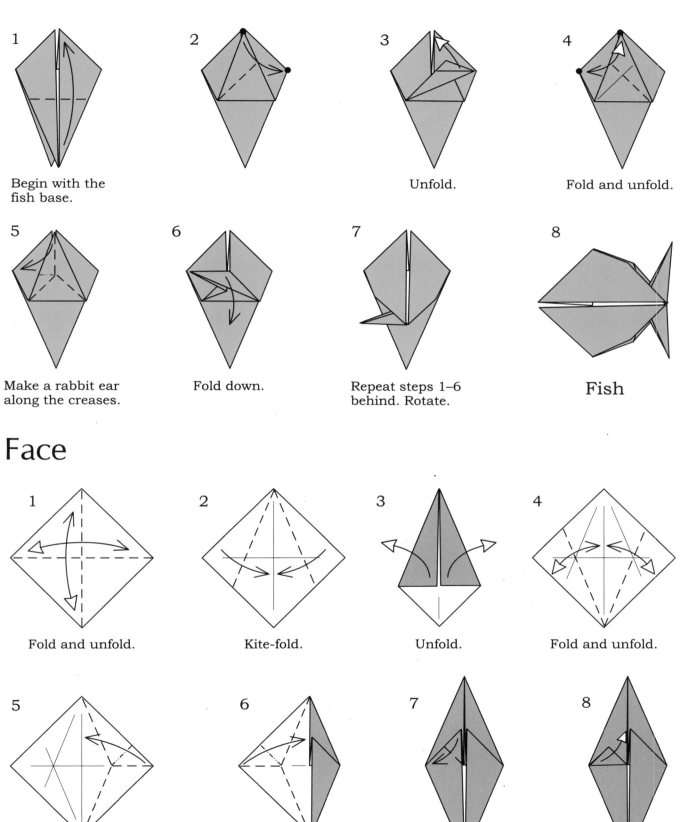

1 Begin with the fish base.

2

3 Unfold.

4 Fold and unfold.

5 Make a rabbit ear along the creases.

6 Fold down.

7 Repeat steps 1–6 behind. Rotate.

8 Fish

Face

1 Fold and unfold.

2 Kite-fold.

3 Unfold.

4 Fold and unfold.

5 Rabbit-ear.

6 Rabbit-ear.

7

8 Unfold.

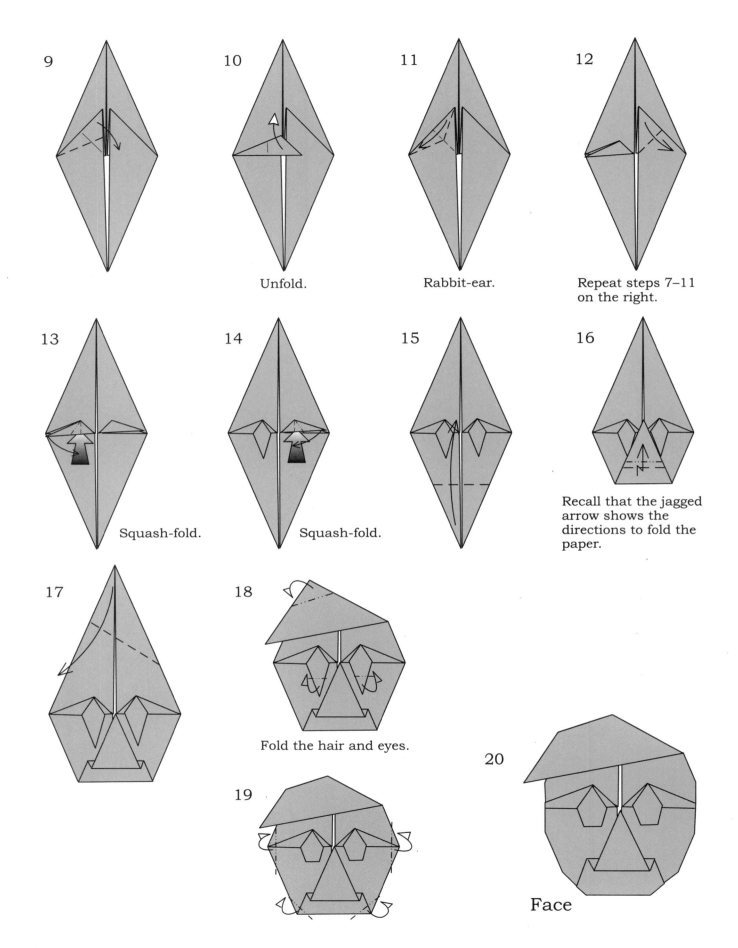

9

10

Unfold.

11

Rabbit-ear.

12

Repeat steps 7–11
on the right.

13

Squash-fold.

14

Squash-fold.

15

16

Recall that the jagged
arrow shows the
directions to fold the
paper.

17

18

Fold the hair and eyes.

19

20

Face

Crimp Fold

A crimp fold is a combination of two reverse folds folded together. They can create a variety of angles and curves; several examples are shown below. Normally you will open the model slightly to form the crimp evenly on each side.

Crimp Folds I

1

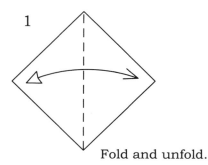

Fold and unfold.

2

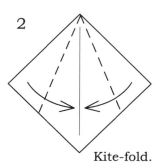

Kite-fold.

3

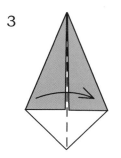

4

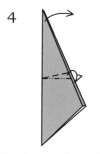

Begin a crimp fold.

5

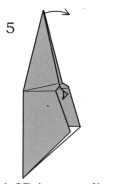
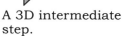

A 3D intermediate step.

6

Crimp-fold.

7

Crimp-fold.

8

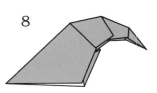

Crimp Folds II

1

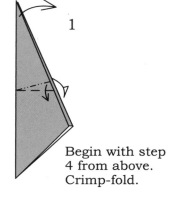

Begin with step 4 from above. Crimp-fold.

2

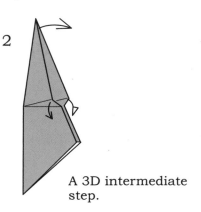

A 3D intermediate step.

3

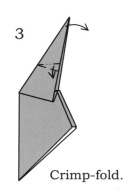

Crimp-fold.

4

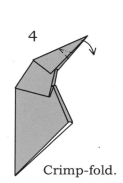

Crimp-fold.

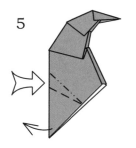

5

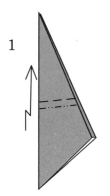

Crimp-fold. This is similar to the reverse folds in the duck's tail.

6

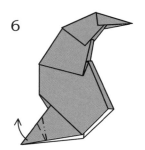

Crimp-fold.

7

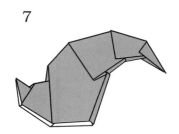

Crimp Folds III

1

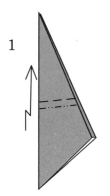

Begin with step 4 from above. Crimp-fold.

2

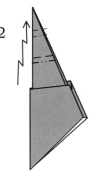

More crimp folds, then rotate.

3

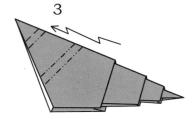

More crimp folds.

4

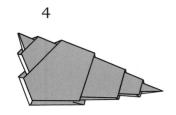

Duck and Swan continued from pages 40 and 41—to add finishing touches.

1

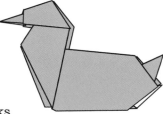

2

Form the beaks with crimp folds.

1

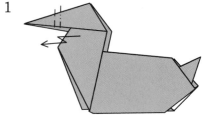

2

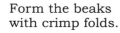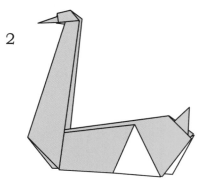

Sink

In a sink fold, some of the paper without edges is folded inside. To do this fold, much of the model must be unfolded.

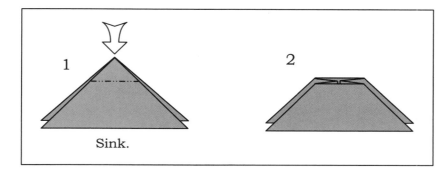

Sink.

Sink Practice Model

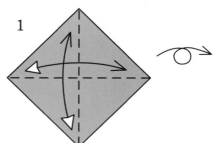

1 Fold and unfold.

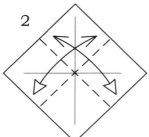

2 Fold and unfold.

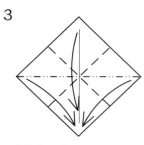

3 Make the preliminary fold.

4 Fold and unfold. Repeat behind.

5 Fold and unfold.

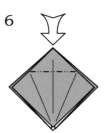

6 Open the model to sink.

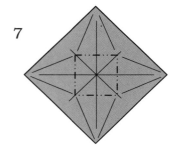

7 The lines in the center square are valley and mountain folds. Make them all become mountain folds. Push the center down into the model. Note that you are changing the direction of each of the folds in the center section so that they can fit inside.

8

Star

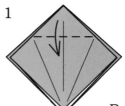

1 Begin with step 5 from above.

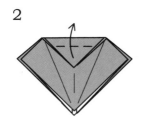

2

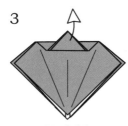

3 Unfold.

4

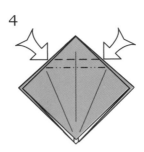

Open the model to
sink down and up.

5

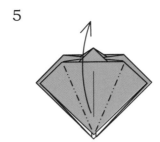

Petal-fold.
Repeat behind.

6

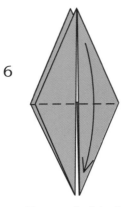

Repeat behind.

7

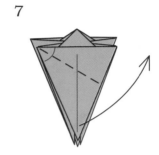

Bisect the angle.

8

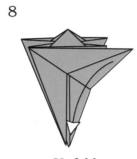

Unfold.

9

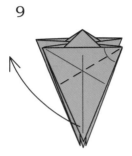

Repeat steps 7–8 in
the other direction.

10

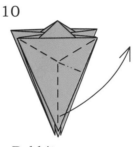

Rabbit-ear.
Repeat behind.

11

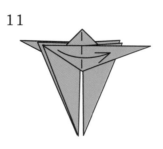

Minor miracle.

12

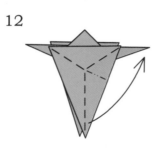

Rabbit-ear.
Repeat behind.

13

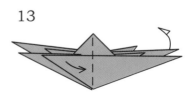

Separate the sides.

14

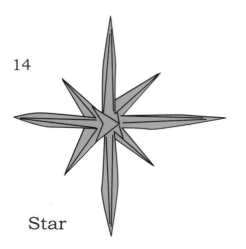

Star

Double Rabbit-Ear

A double rabbit ear is a way to bend and thin a triangular flap. It is often used for making legs. This is much easier than it looks. Once the fold shown in step 5 is started at the top point, the rest of the folding follows naturally.

Double Rabbit-Ear Practice Model

1

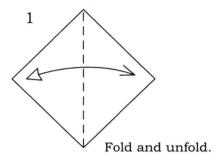

Fold and unfold.

2

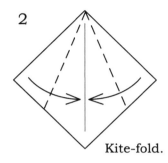

Kite-fold.

3

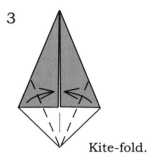

Kite-fold.

4

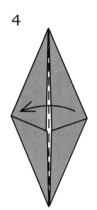

This shape is called the Diamond Base.

5

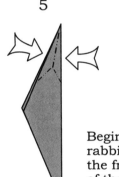

Begin the double rabbit-ear by folding the front and back of the top in half,

6

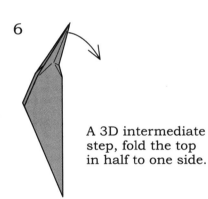

A 3D intermediate step, fold the top in half to one side.

7

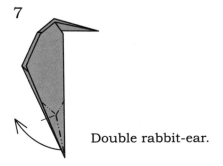

Double rabbit-ear.

8

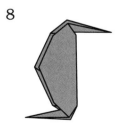

Review

Car

Fold this model to practice making squash folds; ten squash folds are used.

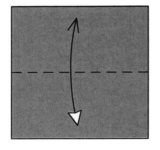

1

Fold and unfold.

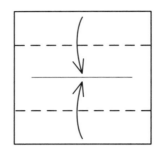

2

Fold to the center.

3

Fold a corner towards the center.

4

Fold the other corners towards the center.

5

Unfold.

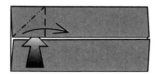

6

Squash-fold.

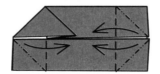

7

Three more squash folds.

8

9

Fold close to the end.

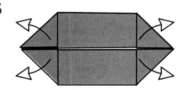

10

Bring the right dot to the left one, which is a bit beyond the edge of the paper.

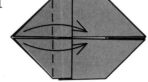

11

12

13

14

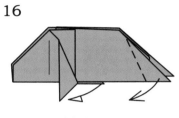 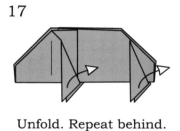

15

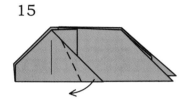

16

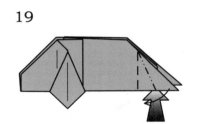

Fold the other
three wheels.

17

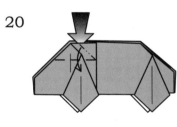

Unfold. Repeat behind.

18

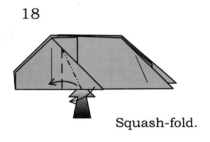

Squash-fold.

19

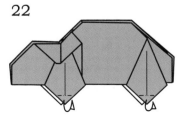

Squash-fold the
other three wheels.

20

Squash-fold.
Repeat behind.

21

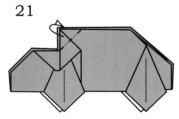

Fold behind.
Repeat behind.

22

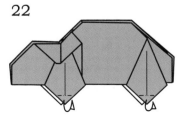

Repeat behind.

23

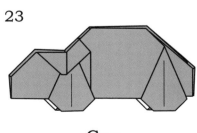

Car

Fish

This model uses many reverse folds. The dotted line in step 16 is used for an x-ray view.

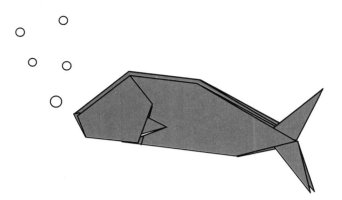

1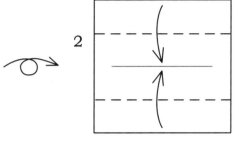

Fold and unfold.

2

Fold to the center.

3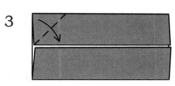

Fold a corner towards the center.

4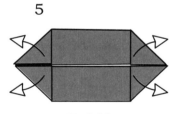

Fold the other corners towards the center.

5

Unfold.

6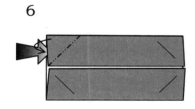

Reverse-fold.

7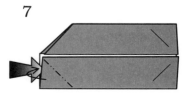

Reverse-fold.

8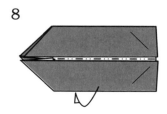

9

Fold the dot to the bottom edge. Repeat behind.

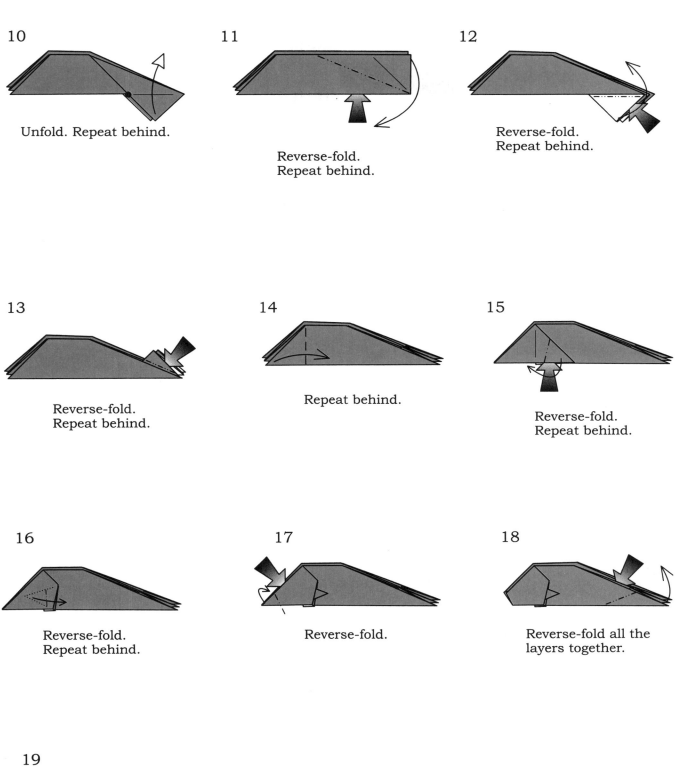

10

Unfold. Repeat behind.

11

Reverse-fold.
Repeat behind.

12

Reverse-fold.
Repeat behind.

13

Reverse-fold.
Repeat behind.

14

Repeat behind.

15

Reverse-fold.
Repeat behind.

16

Reverse-fold.
Repeat behind.

17

Reverse-fold.

18

Reverse-fold all the
layers together.

19

Mountain-fold. Repeat behind.

20

Fish

Three-Headed Moat Monster

This model uses the bird base along
with several outside reverse folds.

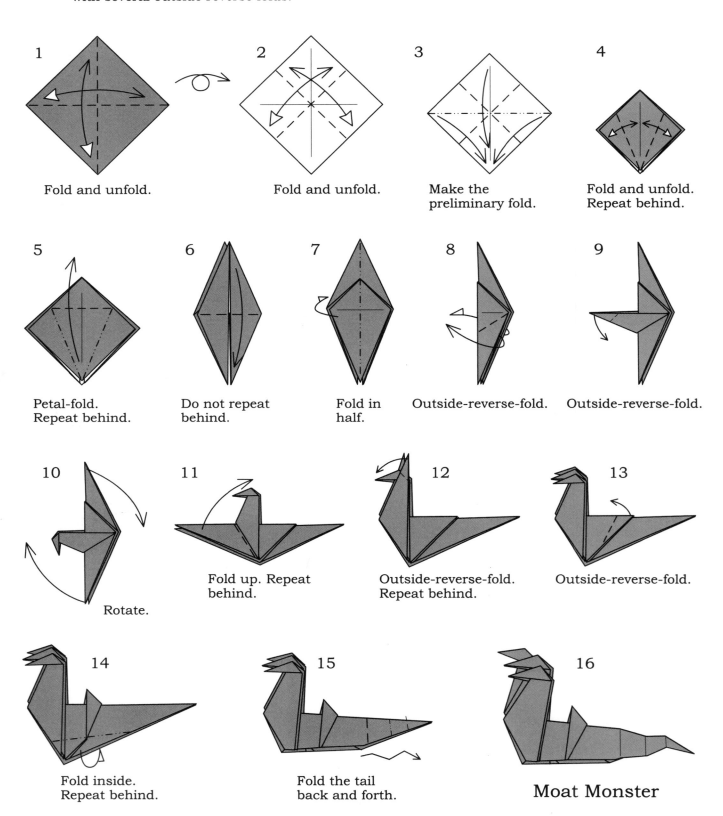

1

Fold and unfold.

2

Fold and unfold.

3

Make the
preliminary fold.

4

Fold and unfold.
Repeat behind.

5

Petal-fold.
Repeat behind.

6

Do not repeat
behind.

7

Fold in
half.

8

Outside-reverse-fold.

9

Outside-reverse-fold.

10

Rotate.

11

Fold up. Repeat
behind.

12

Outside-reverse-fold.
Repeat behind.

13

Outside-reverse-fold.

14

Fold inside.
Repeat behind.

15

Fold the tail
back and forth.

16

Moat Monster

Chapter 2—Intermediate

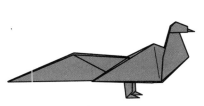

Pheasant

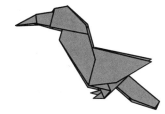

Toucan

Robin

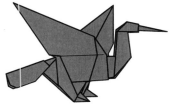

Anhinga

Crane

Canary

These models, all original, build upon the basic folds shown in chapter 1. By folding birds, mammals, and polyhedra, the folder can progress to the next level.

The Pheasant uses several rabbit ears, the Toucan is from the fish base with a sink, the Robin introduces the spread squash fold, and the Anhinga is from the bird base. The "six-sided square" turns into a Crane and the blintz bird base becomes the Canary.

Mammals are very interesting to fold. The Pig, Rabbit, Cat, and Boar show methods for folding legs, ears, and other detail. The spirited Boar has white tusks.

The Tetrahedron, Cube, and Octahedron introduce the new folder to a world of polyhedra. These fascinating geometric shapes reveal different folding techniques.

All these models encourage the folder to realize new potential, enjoyment of origami, and to advance in ability.

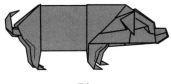

Pig

Rabbit

Cat

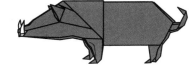

Boar

Tetrahedron

Cube

Octahedron

Pheasant

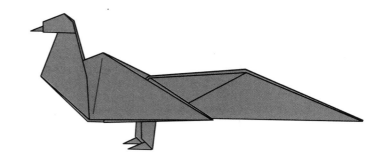

The pheasant uses several rabbit ears and some outside reverse folds. There is also a new fold in step 22.

1

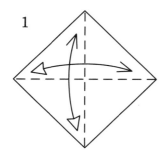

Fold and unfold.

2

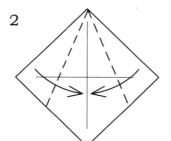

Kite-fold.

3

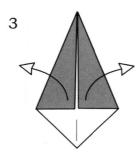

Unfold.

4

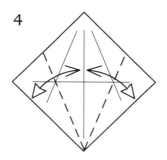

Fold and unfold.

5

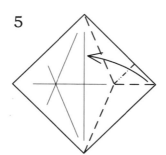

Rabbit-ear.

6

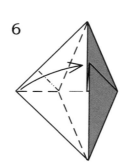

Rabbit-ear.

7

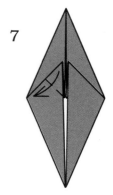

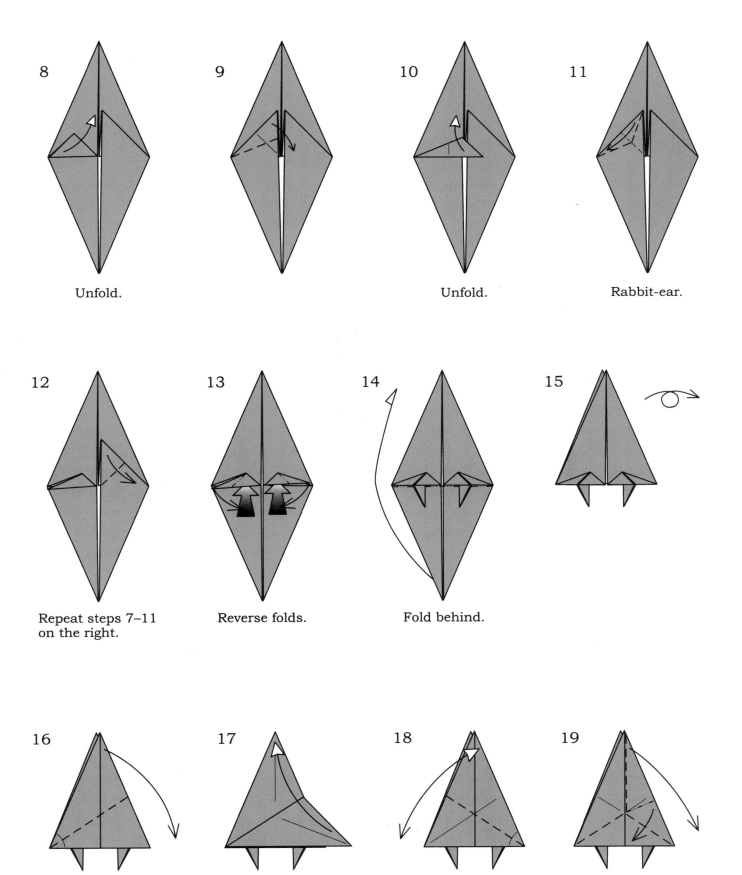

8

Unfold.

9

10

Unfold.

11

Rabbit-ear.

12

Repeat steps 7–11 on the right.

13

Reverse folds.

14

Fold behind.

15

16

Fold down to bisect the angle.

17

Unfold.

18

Fold and unfold.

19

Rabbit-ear.

Pheasant 57

20

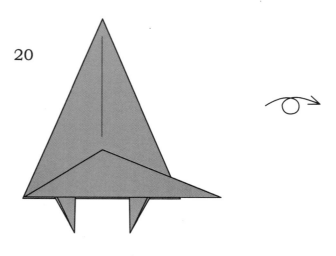

21

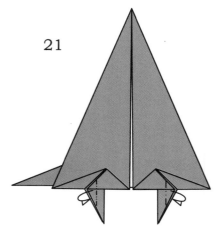

Fold inside and
repeat behind.

22

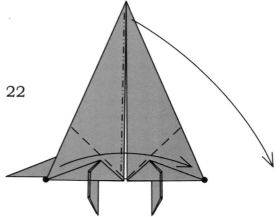

Fold the tail down and to the
right. The dots will meet.

23

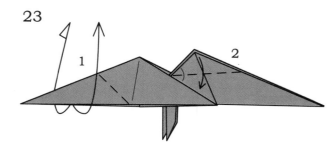

1. Outside-reverse-fold.
2. Fold down and repeat behind.

24

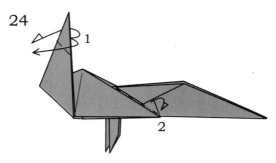

1. Outside-reverse-fold.
2. Fold behind and repeat behind.

25

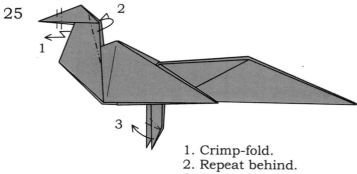

1. Crimp-fold.
2. Repeat behind.
3. Crimp-fold.

26

Pheasant

Toucan

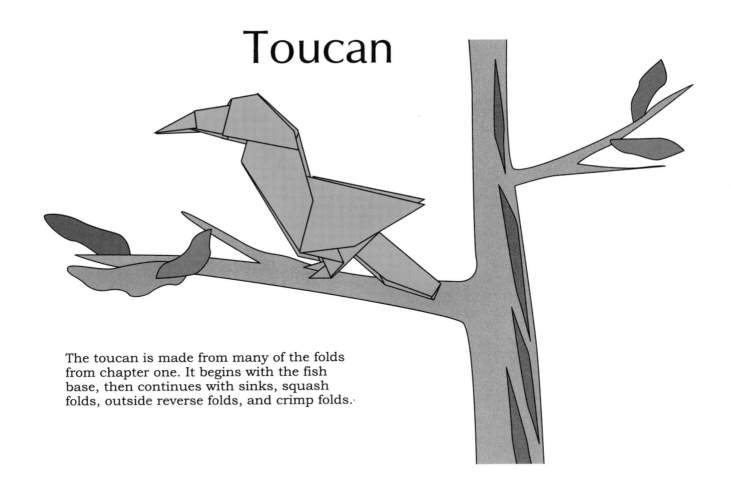

The toucan is made from many of the folds from chapter one. It begins with the fish base, then continues with sinks, squash folds, outside reverse folds, and crimp folds.

1

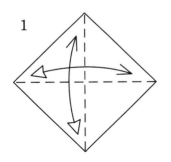

Fold and unfold.

2

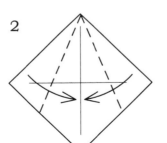

Kite-fold.

3

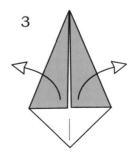

Unfold.

4

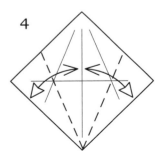

Fold and unfold.

5

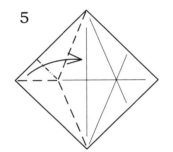

Rabbit-ear.

6

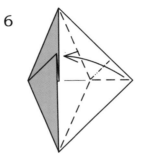

Rabbit-ear.

7

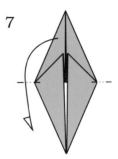

Fold behind.

8

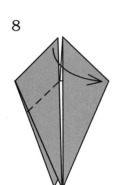

This is the fish base.

9

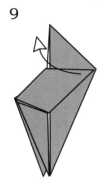

Unfold.

10

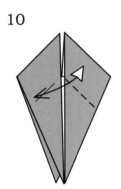

Fold and unfold.

11

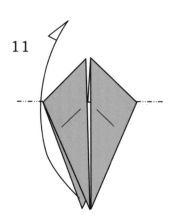

Lift up the back layer.

12

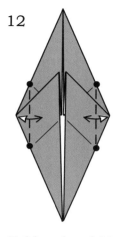

Fold and unfold.

13

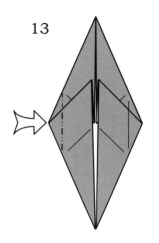

Spread the paper to
make a triangle to sink.

14

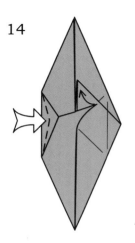

This is a 3D diagram.
Sink the triangle.

15

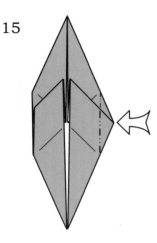

Repeat steps 13–14
on the right.

16

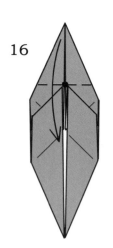

17

18

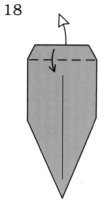

19

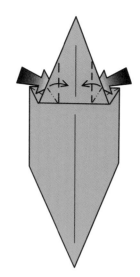

Squash folds.

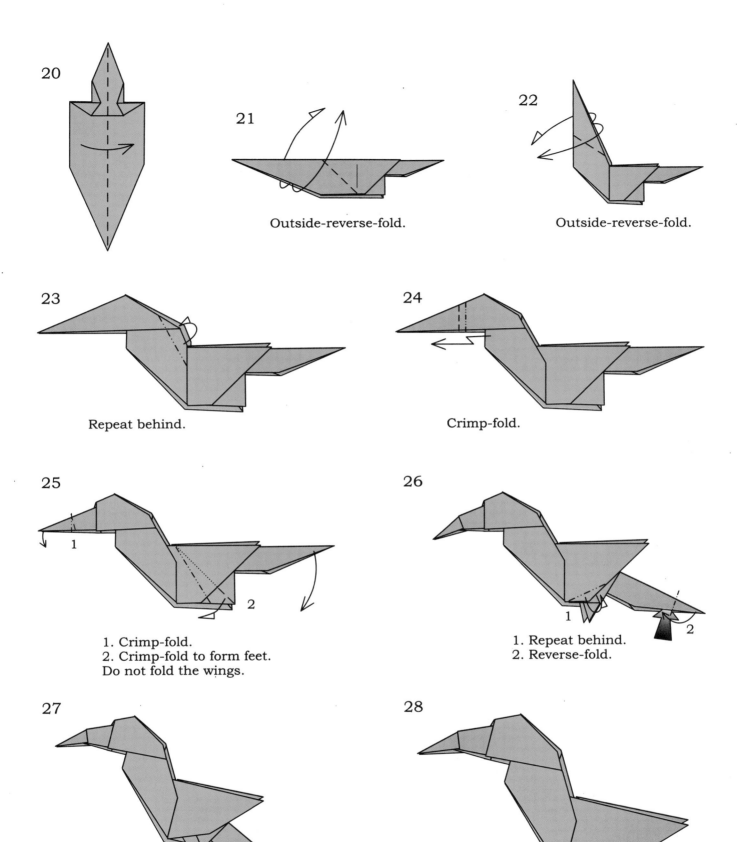

20

21

Outside-reverse-fold.

22

Outside-reverse-fold.

23

Repeat behind.

24

Crimp-fold.

25

1. Crimp-fold.
2. Crimp-fold to form feet.
Do not fold the wings.

26

1. Repeat behind.
2. Reverse-fold.

27

Crimp-fold the feet.

28

Toucan

Robin

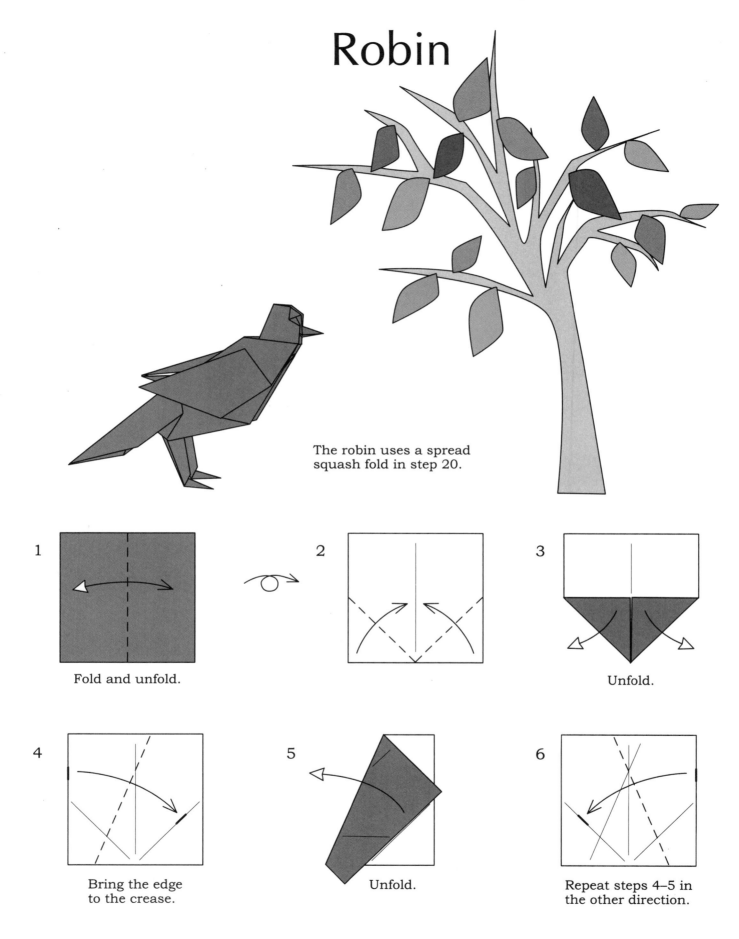

The robin uses a spread squash fold in step 20.

1 Fold and unfold.

2

3 Unfold.

4 Bring the edge to the crease.

5 Unfold.

6 Repeat steps 4–5 in the other direction.

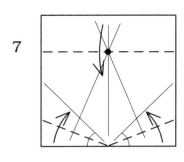

7

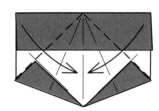

8

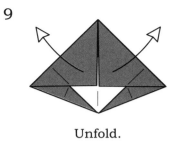

9

Unfold.

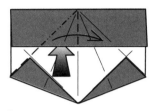

10

Squash-fold.

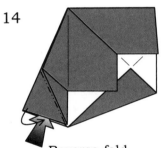

11

Squash-fold.

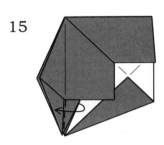

12

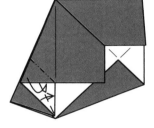

13

Reverse-fold.

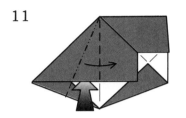

14

Reverse-fold.

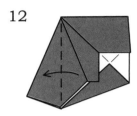

15

Fold the layers together.

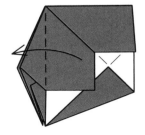

16

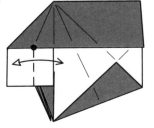

17

Fold and unfold.

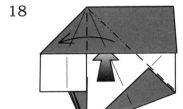

18

Repeat steps 10–17 on the right.

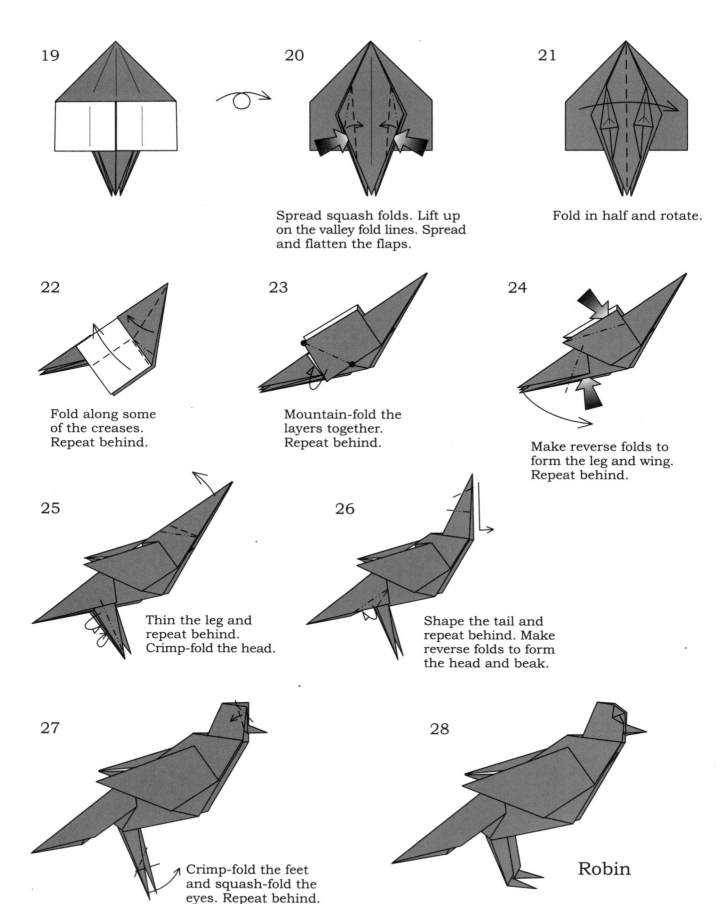

19

20

Spread squash folds. Lift up on the valley fold lines. Spread and flatten the flaps.

21

Fold in half and rotate.

22

Fold along some of the creases. Repeat behind.

23

Mountain-fold the layers together. Repeat behind.

24

Make reverse folds to form the leg and wing. Repeat behind.

25

Thin the leg and repeat behind. Crimp-fold the head.

26

Shape the tail and repeat behind. Make reverse folds to form the head and beak.

27

Crimp-fold the feet and squash-fold the eyes. Repeat behind. The robin can stand.

28

Robin

Anhinga

The anhinga begins with the bird base. The four corners of the square become the head, tail, and wings. The feet are formed from the center.

1

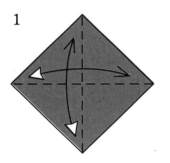

Fold and unfold.

2

Fold and unfold.

3

Make the preliminary fold.

4

Kite-fold. Repeat behind.

5

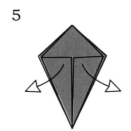

Unfold. Repeat behind.

6

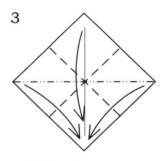

Petal-fold. Repeat behind.

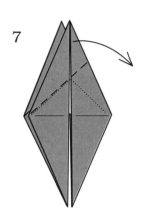

7

Fold the top layer along
the hidden edge.

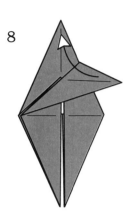

8

Unfold.

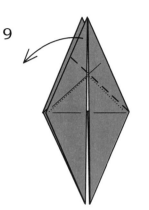

9

Repeat steps 7–8
on the right.

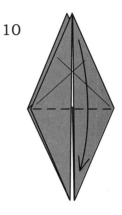

10

Fold down and
repeat behind.

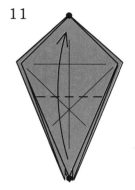

11

Fold the top layer
so the dots meet.

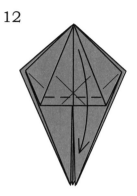

12

Fold the top
layer down.

13

Fold along the creases
on the upper part for
these squash folds.

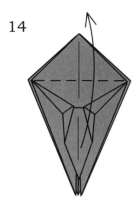

14

Fold up.

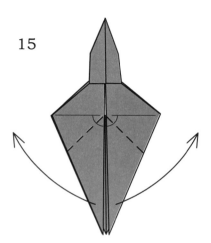

15

Bisect the angles.

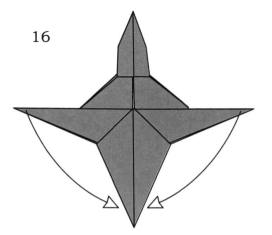

16

Unfold.

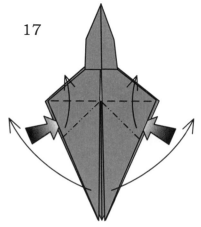

17

Squash folds.

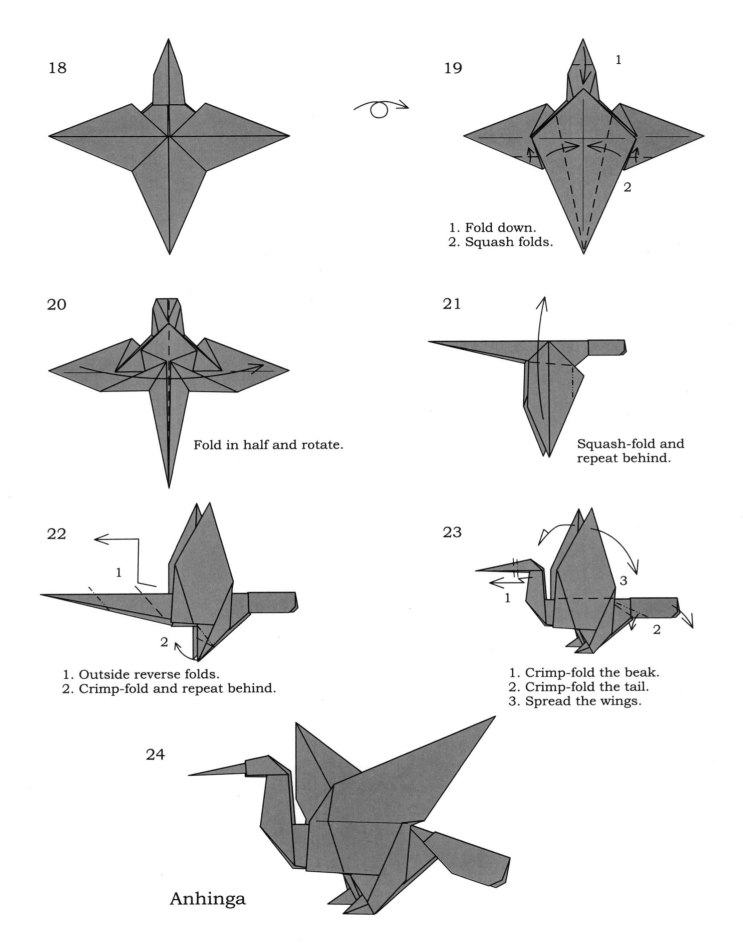

18

19

1. Fold down.
2. Squash folds.

20

Fold in half and rotate.

21

Squash-fold and repeat behind.

22

1. Outside reverse folds.
2. Crimp-fold and repeat behind.

23

1. Crimp-fold the beak.
2. Crimp-fold the tail.
3. Spread the wings.

24

Anhinga

Crane

This crane is a variation of the traditional crane. I developed the six-sided square as a way to form six corners instead of the usual four. In two dimensions it looks like a square with extra paper, but in three dimensions you can see how it is composed of six smaller squares connected at the sides. For this model, the preliminary fold and bird base are formed with two more sides.

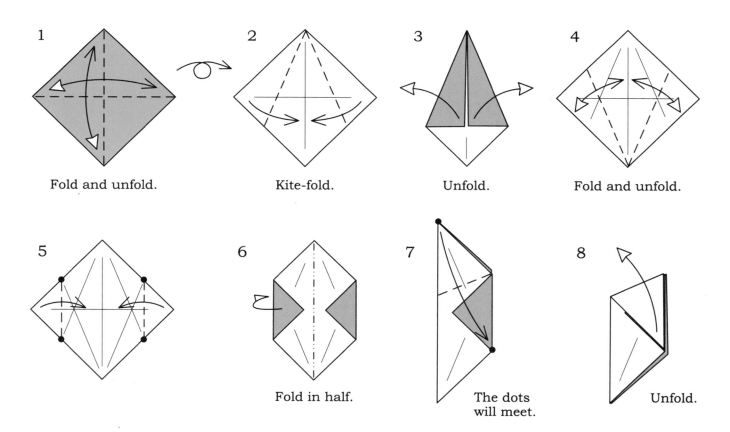

1

Fold and unfold.

2

Kite-fold.

3

Unfold.

4

Fold and unfold.

5

6

Fold in half.

7

The dots will meet.

8

Unfold.

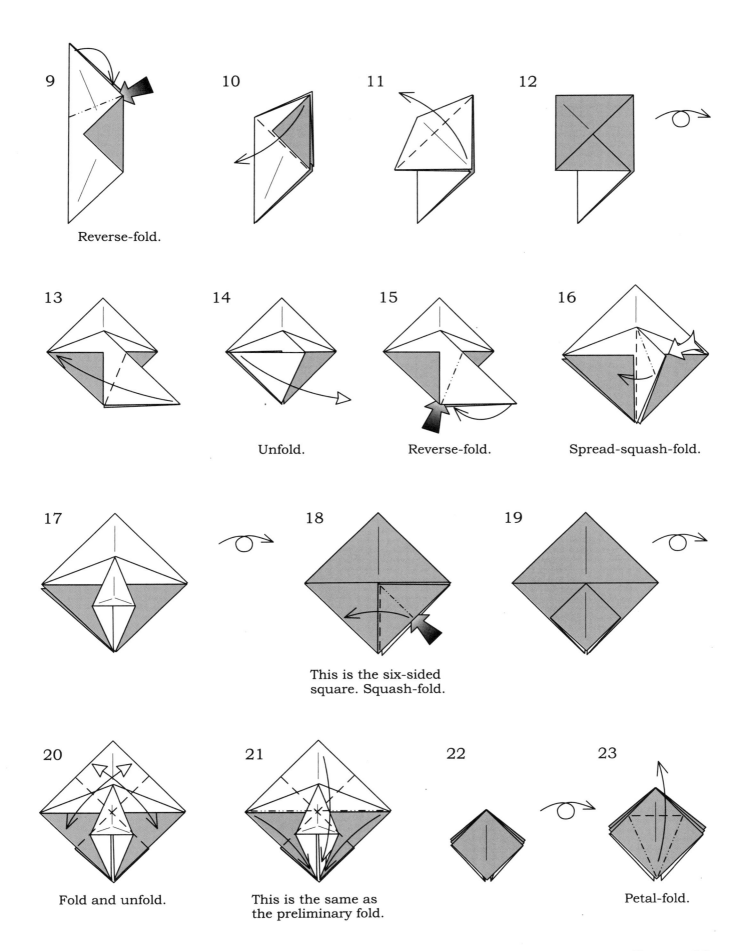

9

Reverse-fold.

10

11

12

13

14

Unfold.

15

Reverse-fold.

16

Spread-squash-fold.

17

18

This is the six-sided
square. Squash-fold.

19

20

Fold and unfold.

21

This is the same as
the preliminary fold.

22

23

Petal-fold.

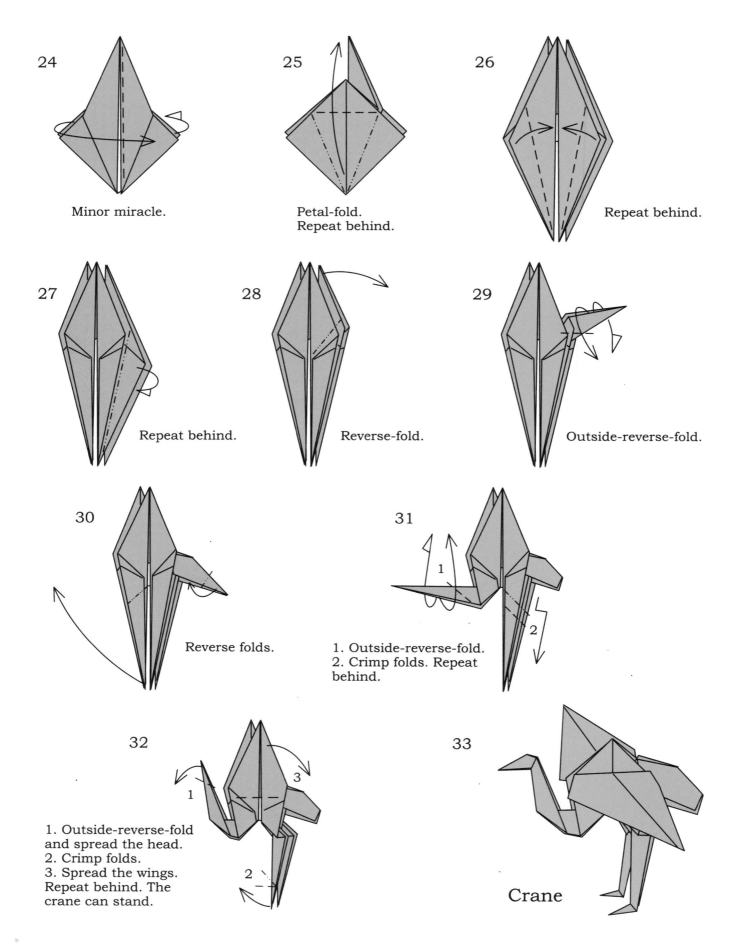

24 Minor miracle.

25 Petal-fold.
Repeat behind.

26 Repeat behind.

27 Repeat behind.

28 Reverse-fold.

29 Outside-reverse-fold.

30 Reverse folds.

31
1. Outside-reverse-fold.
2. Crimp folds. Repeat behind.

32
1. Outside-reverse-fold and spread the head.
2. Crimp folds.
3. Spread the wings. Repeat behind. The crane can stand.

33 Crane

Canary

The canary begins with the blintz bird base, and uses spread squashes and reverse folds.

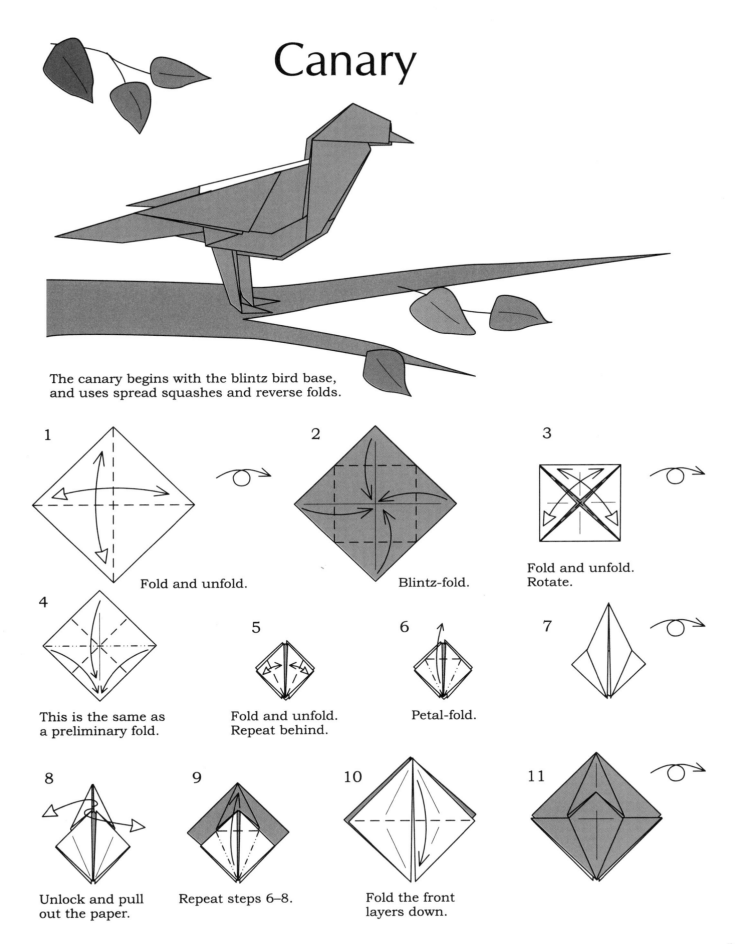

1

Fold and unfold.

2

Blintz-fold.

3

Fold and unfold. Rotate.

4

This is the same as a preliminary fold.

5

Fold and unfold. Repeat behind.

6

Petal-fold.

7

8

Unlock and pull out the paper.

9

Repeat steps 6–8.

10

Fold the front layers down.

11

12

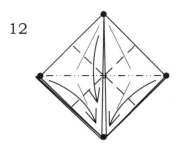

This is similar to the preliminary fold. The dots will meet.

13

Petal-fold.

14

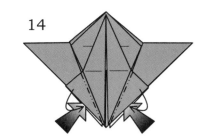

Reverse folds.

15

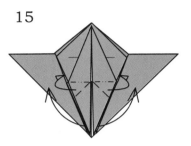

Crimp folds.

16

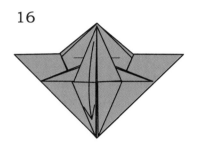

Fold down.

17

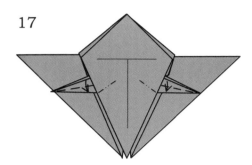

Thin the legs.

18

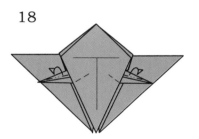

Continue thinning the legs.

19

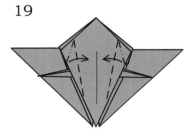

Spread squash folds.

20

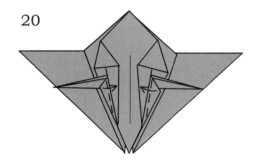

21

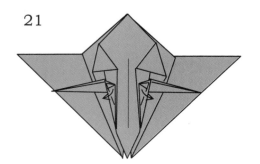

22

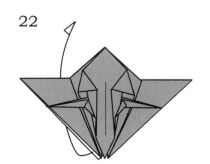

23

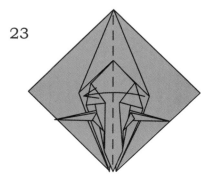

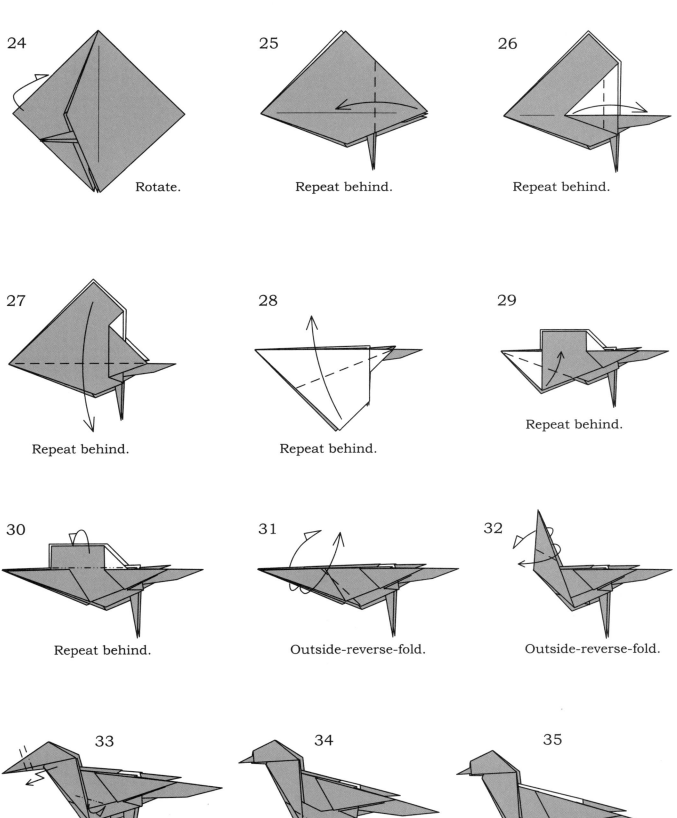

24 Rotate.

25 Repeat behind.

26 Repeat behind.

27 Repeat behind.

28 Repeat behind.

29 Repeat behind.

30 Repeat behind.

31 Outside-reverse-fold.

32 Outside-reverse-fold.

33 Crimp-fold the beak. Repeat behind for the wings.

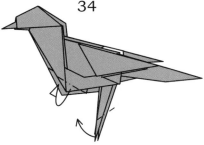

34 Reverse-fold the feet. Repeat behind.

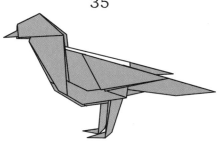

35 Canary

Pig

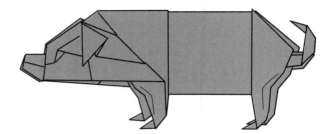

Mammals are among the most difficult of designs to create but luckily they are not so difficult to fold. The pig is formed from a method of folding into a rectangle which makes it possible to form legs in a simple way. It is folded with a seamless closed back, generally considered to be the more realistic and artistic form.

1

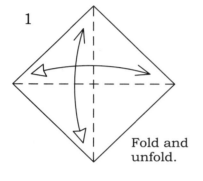

Fold and unfold.

2

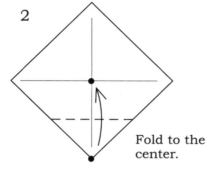

Fold to the center.

3

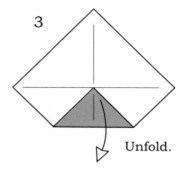

Unfold.

4

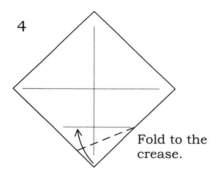

Fold to the crease.

5

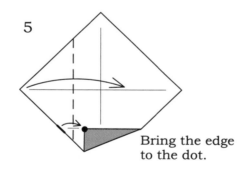

Bring the edge to the dot.

6

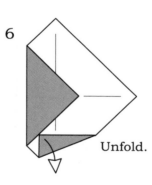

Unfold.

7

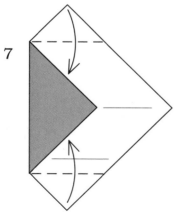

8

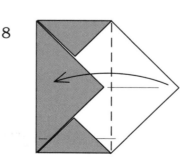

9

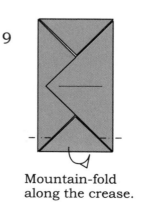

Mountain-fold along the crease.

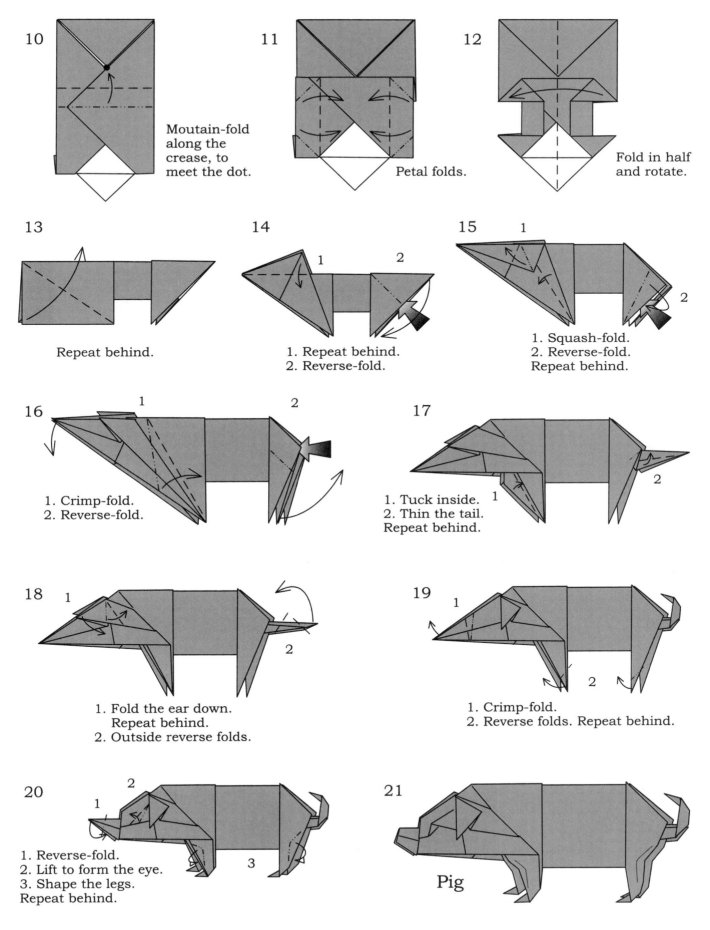

10 Moutain-fold along the crease, to meet the dot.

11 Petal folds.

12 Fold in half and rotate.

13 Repeat behind.

14
1. Repeat behind.
2. Reverse-fold.

15
1. Squash-fold.
2. Reverse-fold.
Repeat behind.

16
1. Crimp-fold.
2. Reverse-fold.

17
1. Tuck inside.
2. Thin the tail.
Repeat behind.

18
1. Fold the ear down.
   Repeat behind.
2. Outside reverse folds.

19
1. Crimp-fold.
2. Reverse folds. Repeat behind.

20
1. Reverse-fold.
2. Lift to form the eye.
3. Shape the legs.
Repeat behind.

21 Pig

Rabbit

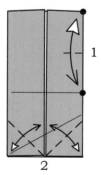

The rabbit uses book-fold symmetry. The ears are formed from several reverse folds.

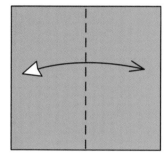

1

Fold and unfold.

2

Fold to the center.

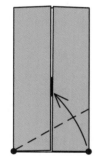

3

Fold the corner to the line.

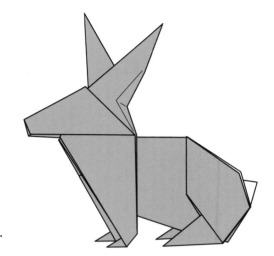

4

Fold behind.

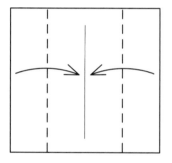

5

Unfold.

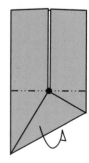

6

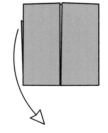

1. Fold and unfold on the right.
2. Fold to the center and unfold.

7

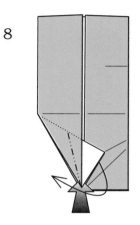

Reverse-fold.

8

Reverse-fold along
a hidden crease.

9

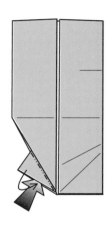

Reverse-fold.

10

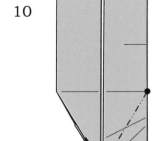

Repeat steps 7–9
on the right.

11

The dots will meet.

12

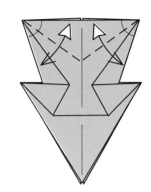

13

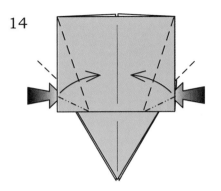

Fold and unfold.

14

Squash folds.

15

Fold and unfold all
the layers. Rotate.

16

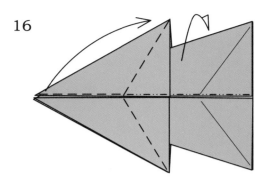

This is similar to a rabbit ear on the left, but the body is folded in half.

17

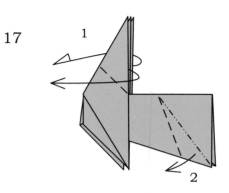

1. Outside-reverse-fold the head.
2. Crimp-fold.

18

1. Reverse-fold the head.
2. Tuck inside.
3. Crimp-fold.
4. Fold one layer behind.
Repeat behind.

19

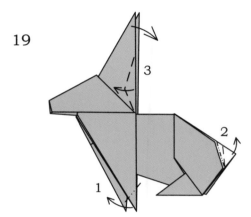

1. Reverse-fold.
2. Crimp-fold.
3. Shape the ears.
Repeat behind.

20

Rabbit

Cat

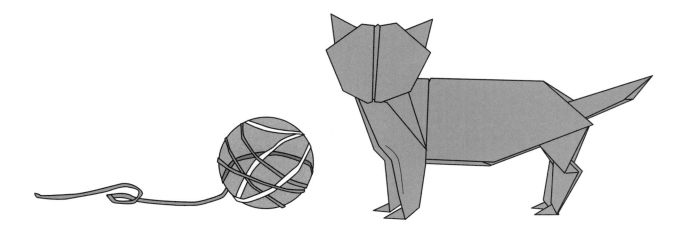

The cat uses another method of folding a
rectangle from which we can form legs in a
simple way.

1
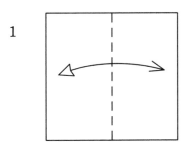

Fold and unfold.

2

Fold to the center.

3
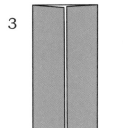

4
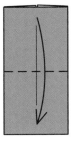

5
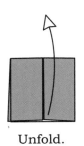

Unfold.

6
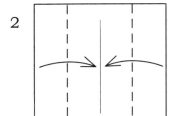

7
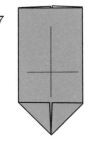

8

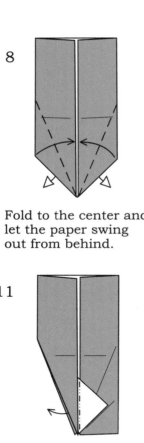

Fold to the center and let the paper swing out from behind.

9

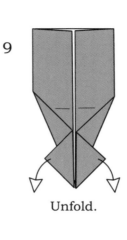

Unfold.

10

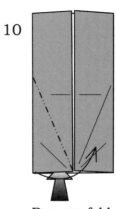

Reverse-fold.

11

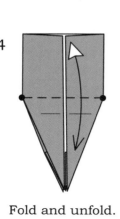

Reverse-fold.

12

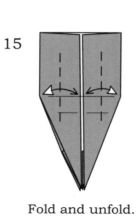

Reverse-fold.

13

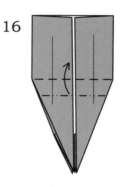

Repeat steps 10–12 on the right.

14

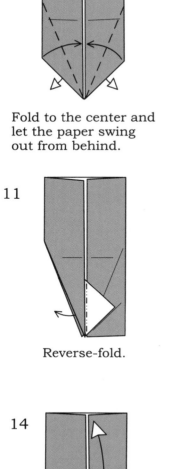

Fold and unfold.

15

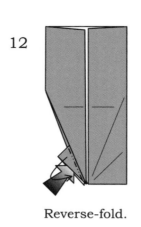

Fold and unfold.

16

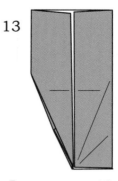

Fold along the creases.

17

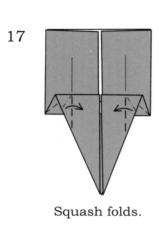

Squash folds.

18

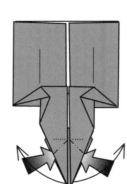

Reverse folds.

19

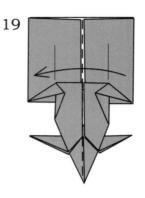

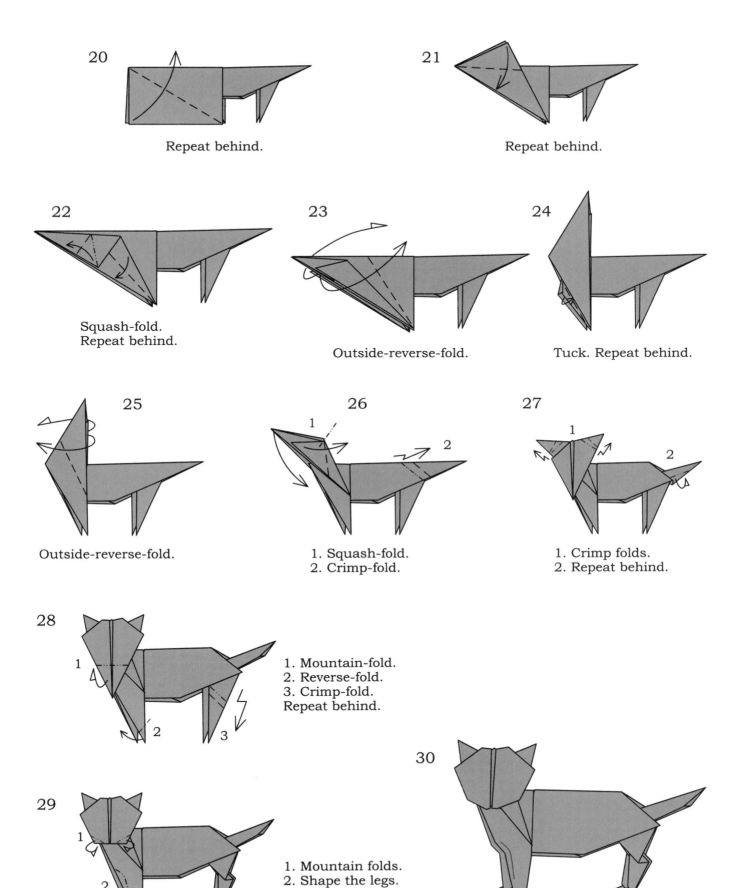

20

Repeat behind.

21

Repeat behind.

22

Squash-fold.
Repeat behind.

23

Outside-reverse-fold.

24

Tuck. Repeat behind.

25

Outside-reverse-fold.

26

1. Squash-fold.
2. Crimp-fold.

27

1. Crimp folds.
2. Repeat behind.

28

1. Mountain-fold.
2. Reverse-fold.
3. Crimp-fold.
Repeat behind.

29

1. Mountain folds.
2. Shape the legs.
3. Crimp-fold.
Repeat behind.

30

Cat

Boar

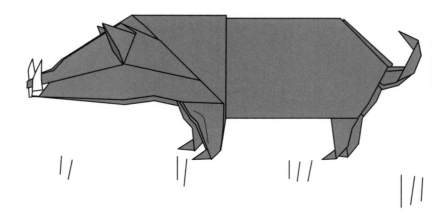

The boar begins in a similar way to the cat.
Two corners become the tusks, then the
folding continues as in the pig.

1

Fold and unfold.

2

Fold to the center.

3

4

5

Unfold.

6

7

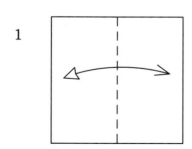 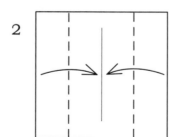 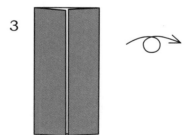

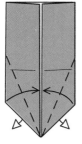

8

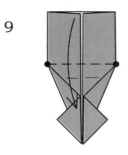

9

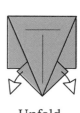

10

Fold to the center and
let the paper swing
out from behind.

Unfold.

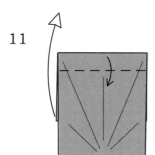

11

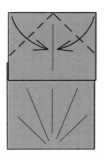

12

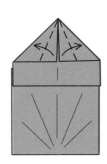

13

Flip up the back
while folding along
the crease.

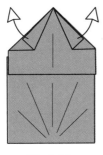

14

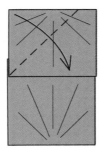

15

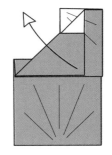

16

Unfold.

Unfold.

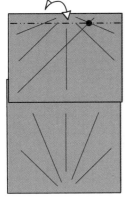

17

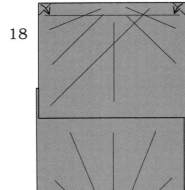

18

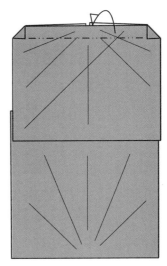

19

Fold and unfold.

Tuck inside.

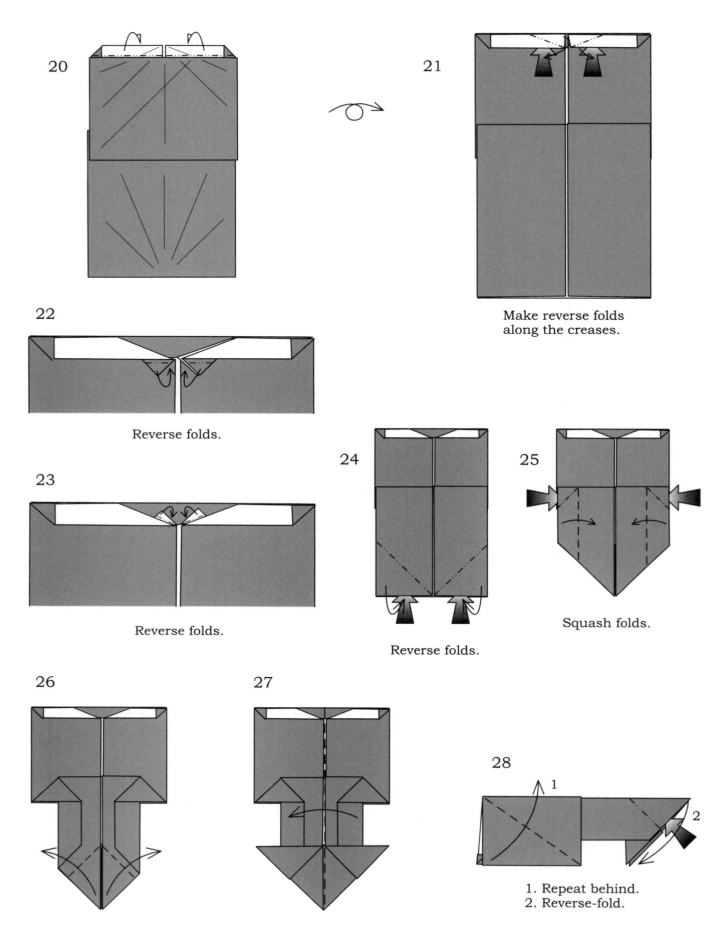

20

21

Make reverse folds
along the creases.

22

Reverse folds.

23

Reverse folds.

24

Reverse folds.

25

Squash folds.

26

27

28

1. Repeat behind.
2. Reverse-fold.

29

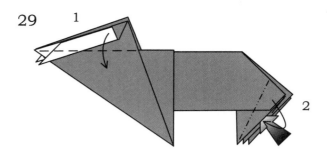

1. Repeat behind.
2. Reverse-fold. Repeat behind.

30

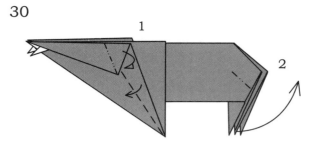

1. Fold inside. Repeat behind.
2. Reverse-fold.

31

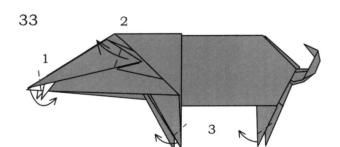

1. Crimp-fold.
2. Thin the tail. Repeat behind.

32

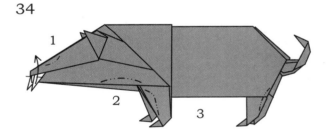

1. Tuck, repeat behind.
2. Outside reverse folds.

33

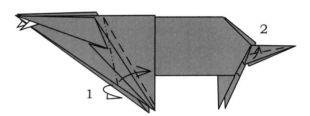

1. Reverse-fold.
2. Repeat behind.
3. Reverse folds. Repeat behind.

34

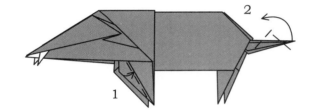

Shape the tusks, head, and legs. Repeat behind.

35

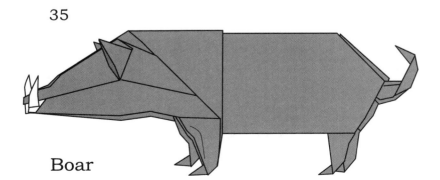

Boar

Tetrahedron

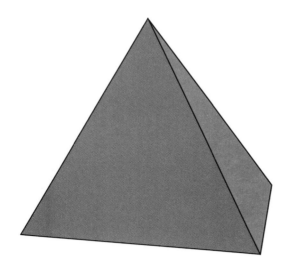

Origami polyhedra require a different style of folding. All the folds are exact with landmarks. Some of the creases are on small line segments. Assembling the final shape with possible locks is interesting.

Composed of four equilateral triangles, the tetrahedron is the simplest of the five Platonic solids. Plato believed the tetrahedron represented fire because of its sharpness and simplicity.

1
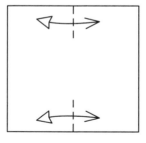
Fold and unfold on the edges.

2
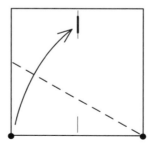
Bring the corner to the crease.

3
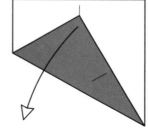
Unfold.

4
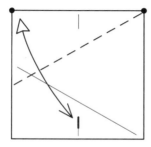
Fold and unfold.

5
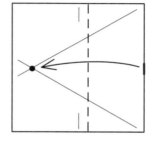
Bring the edge to the dot.

6
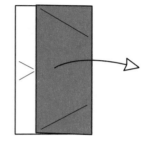
Unfold.

7

Fold along the crease.

8

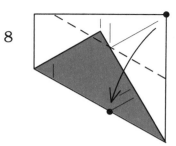

The dots will meet.

9

10

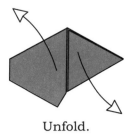

Unfold.

11

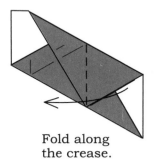

Fold along
the crease.

12

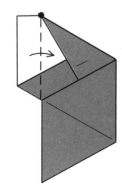

13

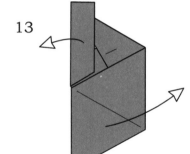

Unfold.

14

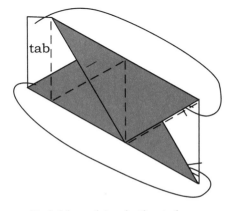

tab

Refold and tuck the tab
inside. Then crease along
the edges of the tetrahedron.

15

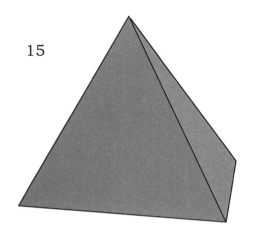

Tetrahedron

Cube

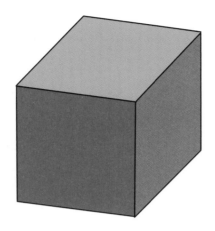

Much of the folding for this cube is done while the model is three dimensional. Three flaps lock the model. Plato believed this regular polyhedron, composed of six squares, symbolized earth because of its stability.

1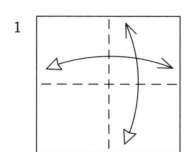

Fold and unfold.

2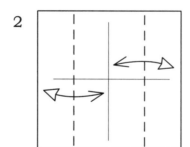

Fold and unfold.

3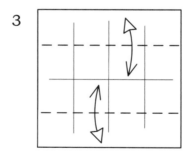

Fold and unfold.

4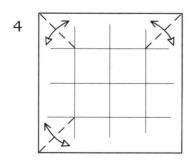

Fold and unfold.

5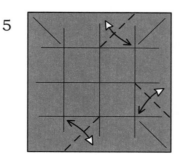

Fold and unfold.

6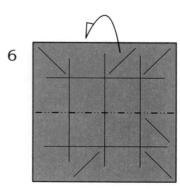

Fold in half.

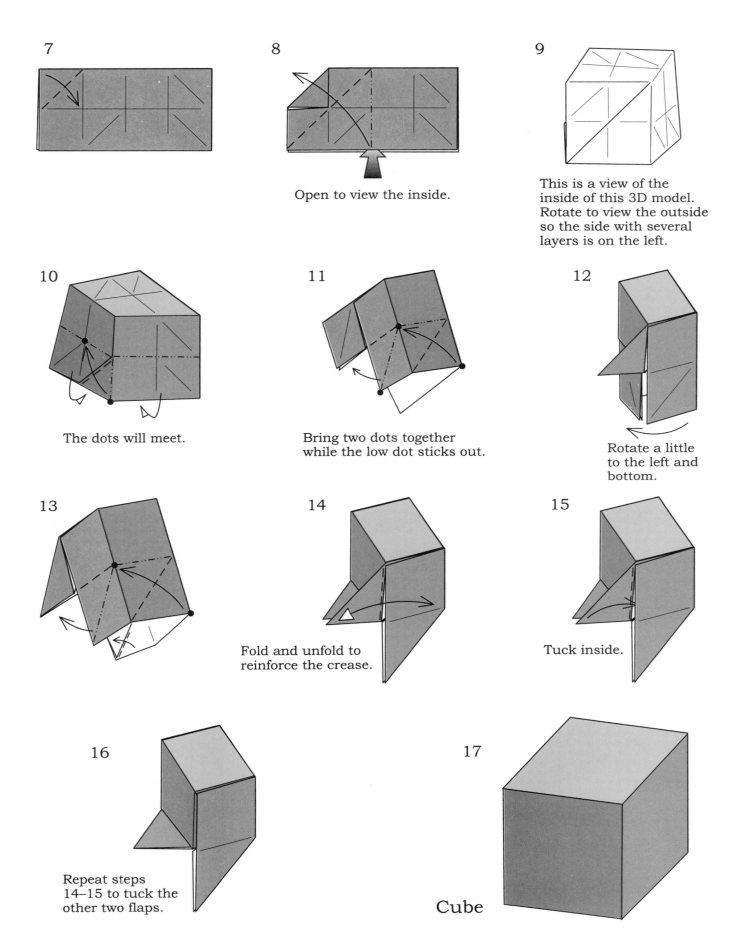

7

8

Open to view the inside.

9

This is a view of the inside of this 3D model. Rotate to view the outside so the side with several layers is on the left.

10

The dots will meet.

11

Bring two dots together while the low dot sticks out.

12

Rotate a little to the left and bottom.

13

14

Fold and unfold to reinforce the crease.

15

Tuck inside.

16

Repeat steps 14–15 to tuck the other two flaps.

17

Cube

Octahedron

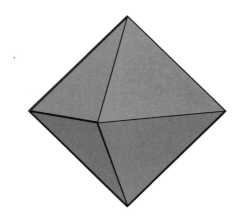

All the folds for this octahedron are two dimensional until the last step when it is inflated. This regular polyhedron, formed from eight equilateral triangles, represented air to Plato because it appears to be suspended.

1
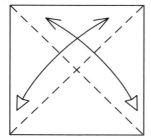
Fold and unfold.

2
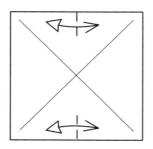
Fold and unfold on the edges.

3
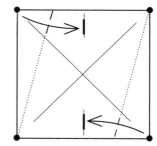
Crease at the top and bottom.

4
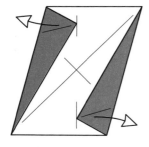
Unfold.

5
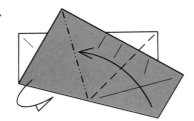
Fold and unfold on the edges.

6
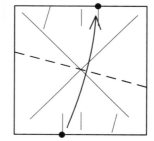

7

8

Turn over and repeat.

9
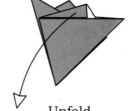
Unfold.

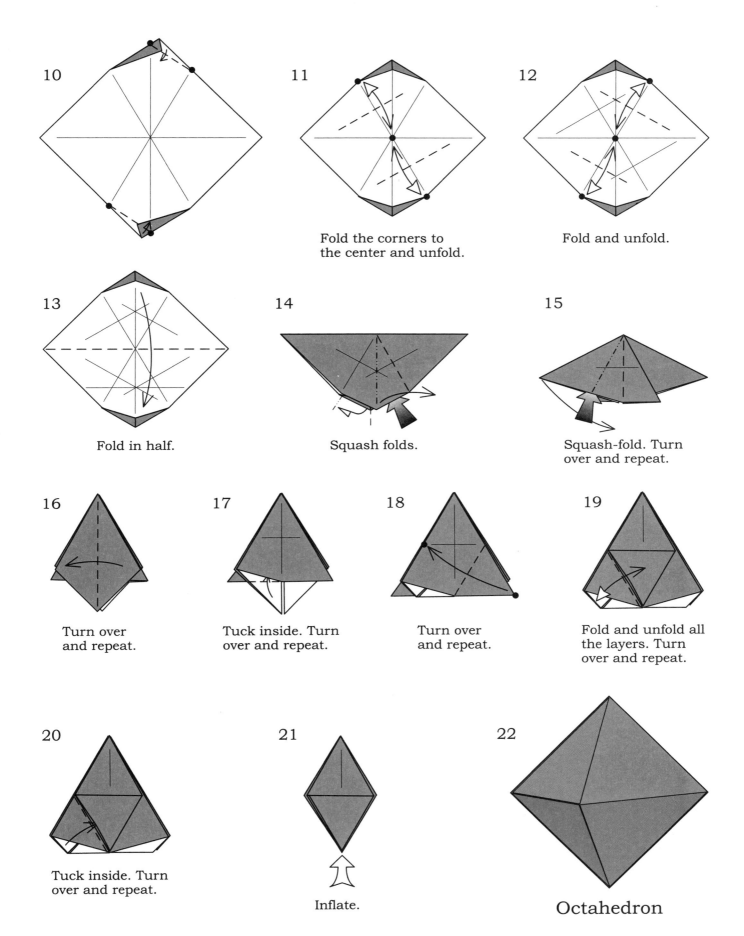

10

11
Fold the corners to
the center and unfold.

12
Fold and unfold.

13
Fold in half.

14
Squash folds.

15
Squash-fold. Turn
over and repeat.

16
Turn over
and repeat.

17
Tuck inside. Turn
over and repeat.

18
Turn over
and repeat.

19
Fold and unfold all
the layers. Turn
over and repeat.

20
Tuck inside. Turn
over and repeat.

21
Inflate.

22
Octahedron

Chapter 3—Advanced

Fred Rohm's Impossible Vase

Bee

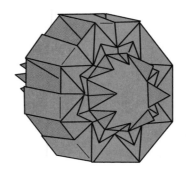

Fred Rohm's Water Wheel

You are now ready to fold advanced models. These have more folds including many difficult steps. Fold slowly and accurately. It might be easier to use larger paper, such as 10 inch squares.

Two of Fred Rohm's models are shown—his Impossible Vase and Water Wheel. They make for very satisfying three dimensional folding. You can tell by the folding methods that there must be many ways to fold these.

Then come some of my models. The Deer is from a half blintz base. The front legs come from the center of the paper allowing for more paper in the antlers. There are challenging folds to make the Elephant with such details as white tusks. The Bee is from the double blintz bird base to give it all its points.

Being able to fold these advanced models is a sign of mastery with origami.

Deer

Elephant

Fred Rohm's Impossible Vase

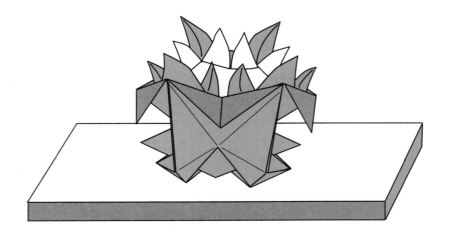

Fred Rohm created this vase as a challenge with folder/creator Neal Elias. The challenge was to come up with as many points as possible. Though not impossible to fold, it was titled the impossible vase because it had more points than previously thought possible.

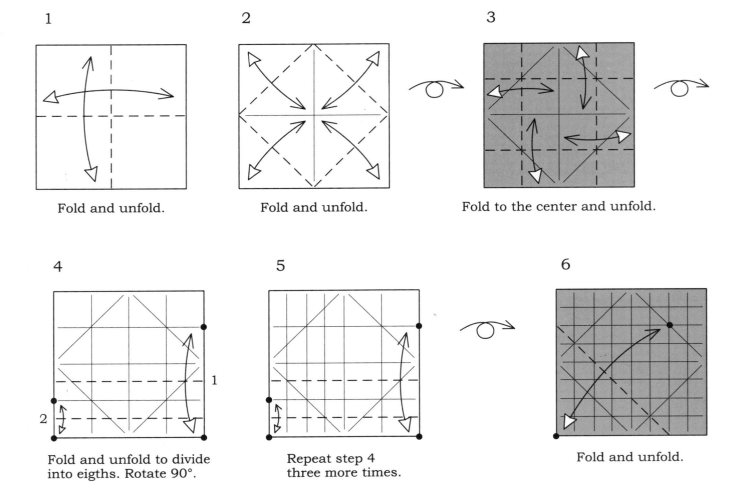

1

Fold and unfold.

2

Fold and unfold.

3

Fold to the center and unfold.

4

Fold and unfold to divide into eigths. Rotate 90°.

5

Repeat step 4 three more times.

6

Fold and unfold.

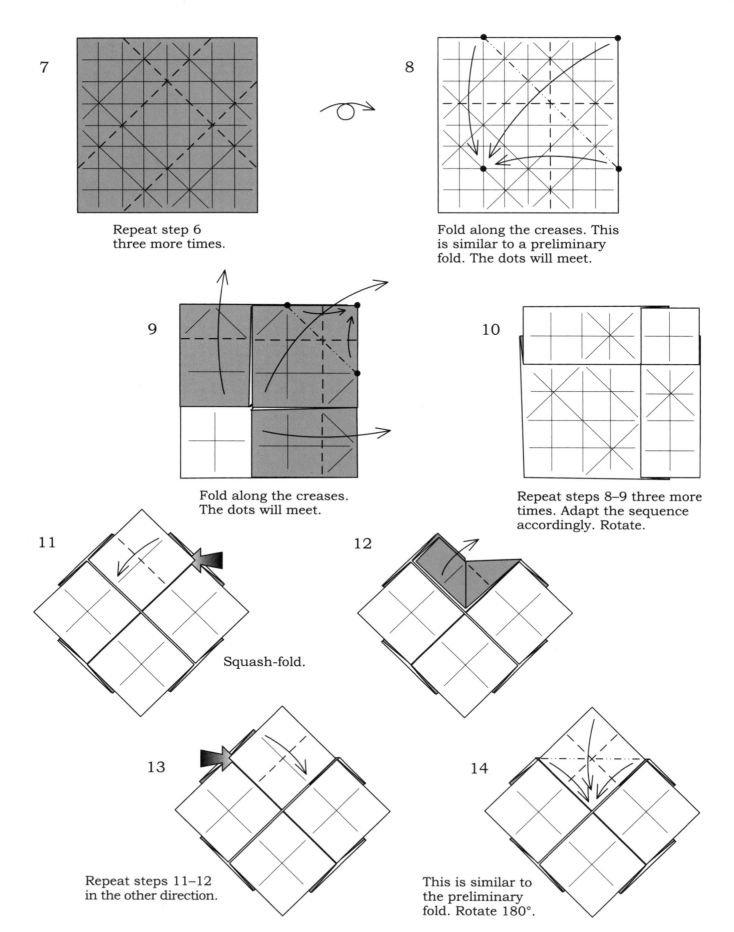

7

Repeat step 6
three more times.

8

Fold along the creases. This
is similar to a preliminary
fold. The dots will meet.

9

Fold along the creases.
The dots will meet.

10

Repeat steps 8–9 three more
times. Adapt the sequence
accordingly. Rotate.

11

Squash-fold.

12

13

Repeat steps 11–12
in the other direction.

14

This is similar to
the preliminary
fold. Rotate 180°.

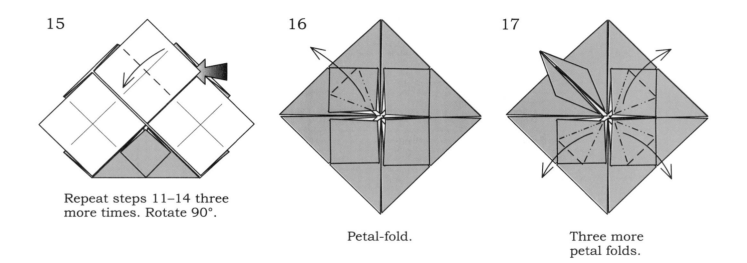

15

Repeat steps 11–14 three
more times. Rotate 90°.

16

Petal-fold.

17

Three more
petal folds.

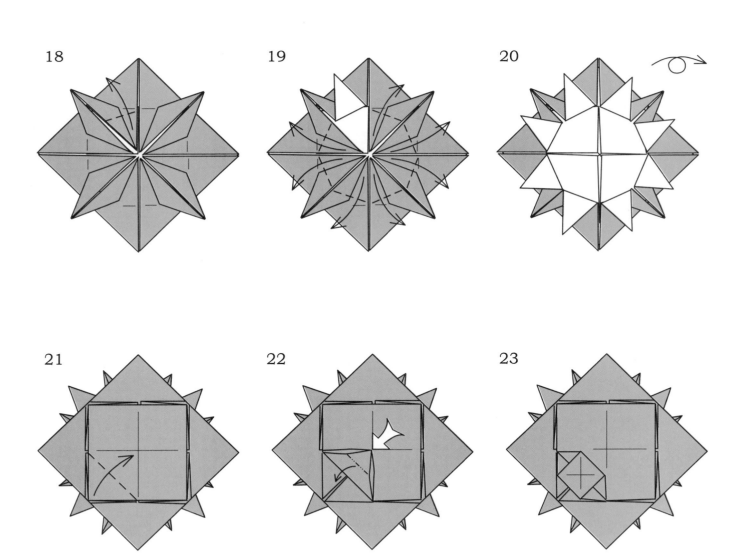

18

19

20

21

22

Spread-squash-fold.

23

Repeat steps 21–22 on
the three other sides.

24

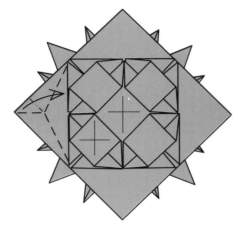

Rabbit-ear.

25

Rabbit-ear on the three other sides.

26

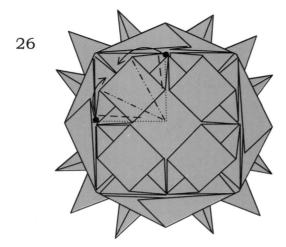

Fold the corners with the dots towards each other. This will become the stand and the model will be 3D.

27

This is 3D. Continue step 26 on the three other sides.

28

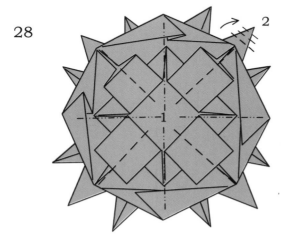

This is 3D.
1. Shape the vase so it will stand but keep the base flat.
2. Curl the flaps all around.

29

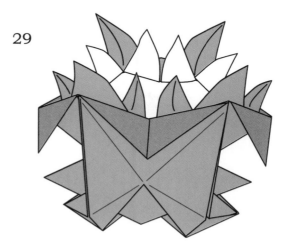

Fred Rohm's Impossible Vase

Fred Rohm's Water Wheel

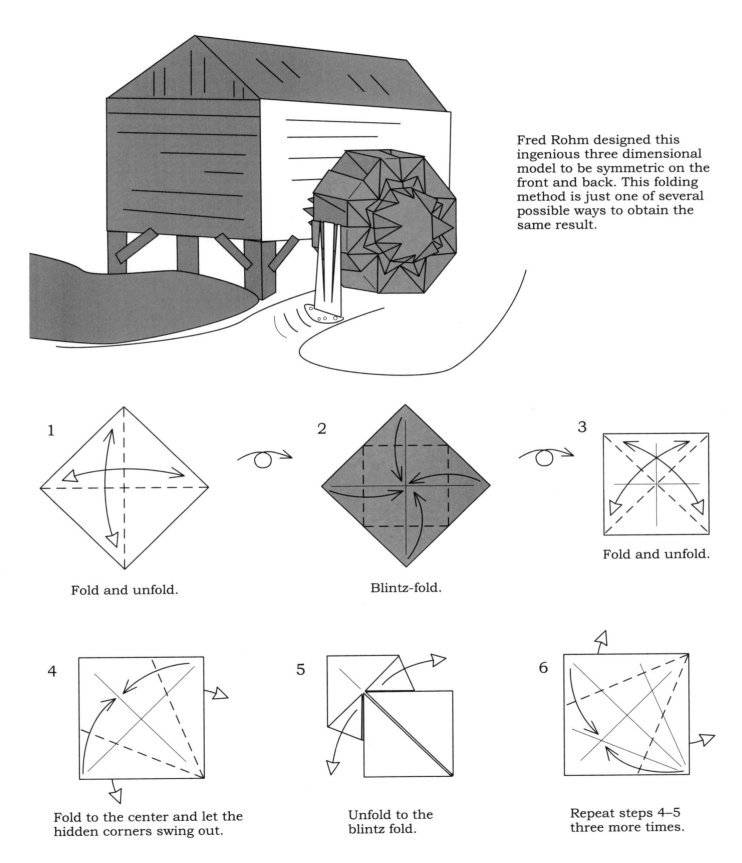

Fred Rohm designed this ingenious three dimensional model to be symmetric on the front and back. This folding method is just one of several possible ways to obtain the same result.

1

Fold and unfold.

2

Blintz-fold.

3

Fold and unfold.

4

Fold to the center and let the hidden corners swing out.

5

Unfold to the blintz fold.

6

Repeat steps 4–5 three more times.

7

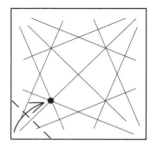

Fold to the dot.

8

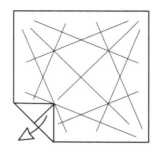

Unfold.

9

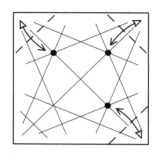

Fold and unfold.

10

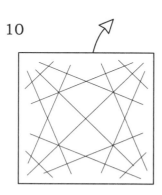

Unfold everything.

11

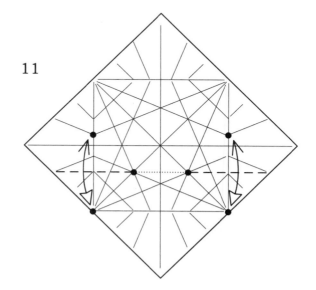

Fold and unfold but not
in the center. Rotate 90°.

12

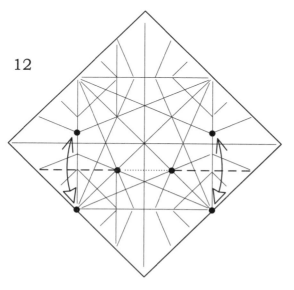

Repeat step 11 three
more times. Rotate.

13

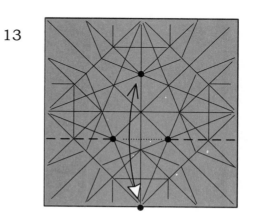

Fold and unfold but not
in the center. Rotate 90°.

14

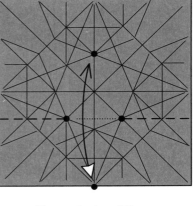

Repeat step 13
three more times.

15

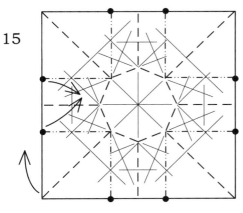

Now the fun begins. Only fold along
the creases. Begin by folding along
the octagon in the center. The
octagon will remain flat, at the
bottom, and all the rest of the paper
will go up. Fold all the corners in
half while lifting up. All the dots will
meet at the top. The arrows show
only a part of the entire step.

16

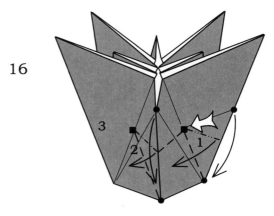

Only fold along creases in this 3D step to
flatten it.
1. Push in at the little square so the dots
on the right meet.
2. While making the model flat, the two
small squares will meet. The two center
dots will meet.
3. This is the same as 1, continue spiraling
all around. All the eight little squares will
meet in the center. The eight pairs of dots
will meet on the bottom octagon.

17

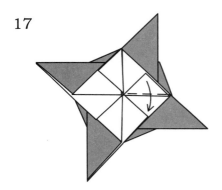

18

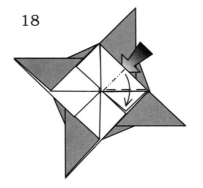

Squash-fold in 3D.

19

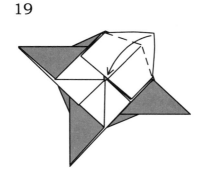

Flatten this 3D step.

20

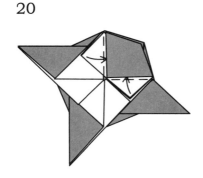

Tuck inside.

Fred Rohm's Water Wheel 99

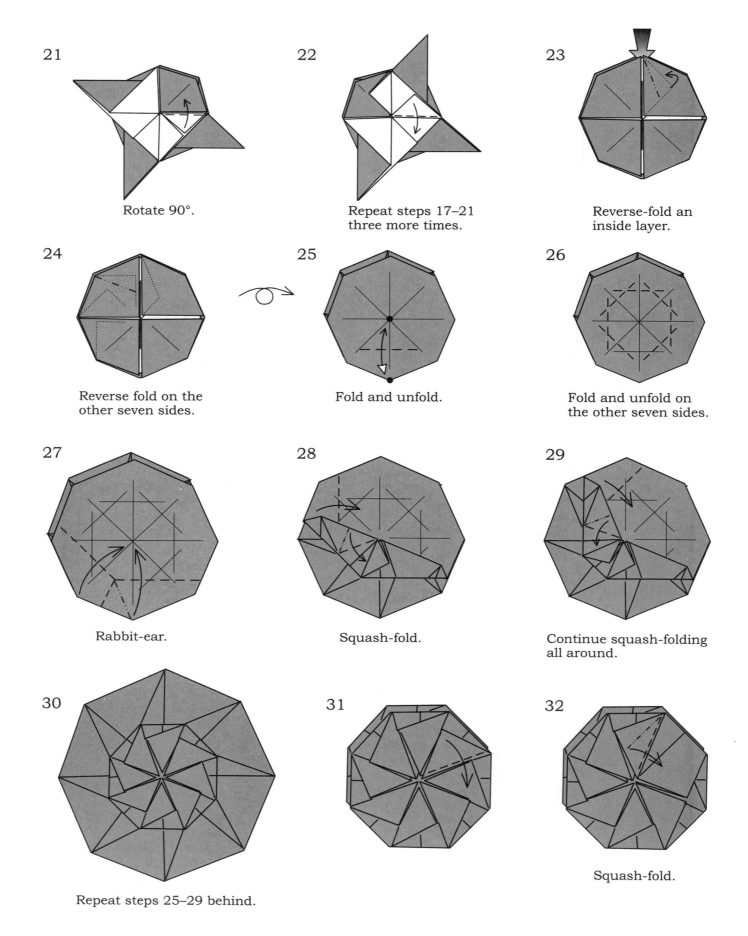

21

Rotate 90°.

22

Repeat steps 17–21 three more times.

23

Reverse-fold an inside layer.

24

Reverse fold on the other seven sides.

25

Fold and unfold.

26

Fold and unfold on the other seven sides.

27

Rabbit-ear.

28

Squash-fold.

29

Continue squash-folding all around.

30

Repeat steps 25–29 behind.

31

32

Squash-fold.

33

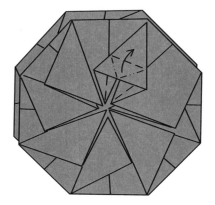

Petal-fold.

34

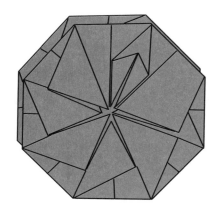

Repeat steps 32–32 on the seven other sides.

35

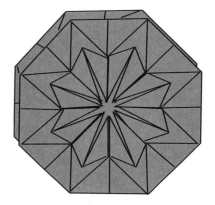

Repeat steps 31–34 behind.

36

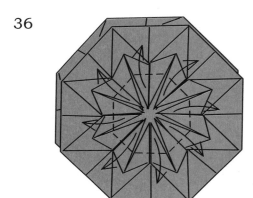

Fold these corners out. Repeat behind.

37

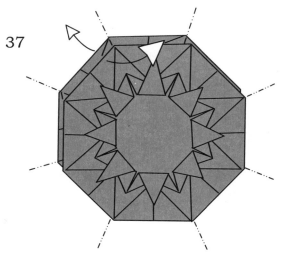

Separate the front and back while creasing the eight middle edges.

38

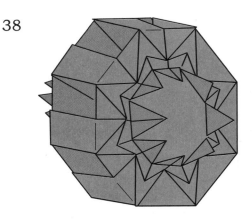

Fred Rohm's Water Wheel

Deer

The deer begins with a half blintz base and a sink. Two corners form the antlers, and the front legs come from the center of the paper.

1

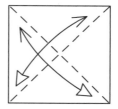

Fold and unfold.

2

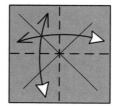

Fold and unfold.

3

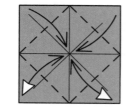

Blintz-fold and unfold at the bottom.

4

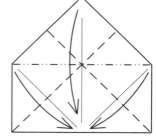

This is similar to the waterbomb base.

5

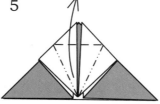

Petal-fold.

6

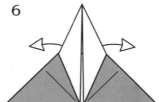

Pull out the hidden corners.

7

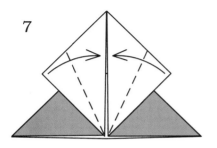

Kite-fold.

8

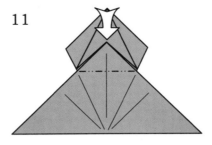

9

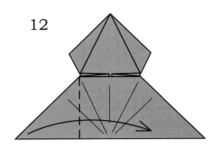

Fold and unfold
the triangle.

10

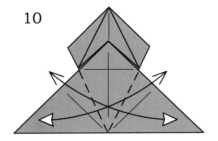

Fold and unfold.

11

Sink.

12

13

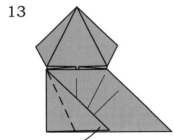

14

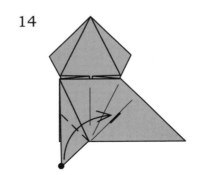

15

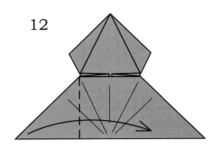

16

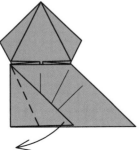

Unfold.

17

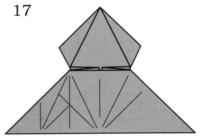

Repeat steps 12–16
on the right.

18

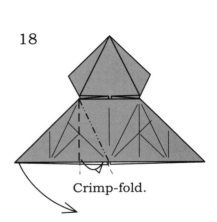

Crimp-fold.

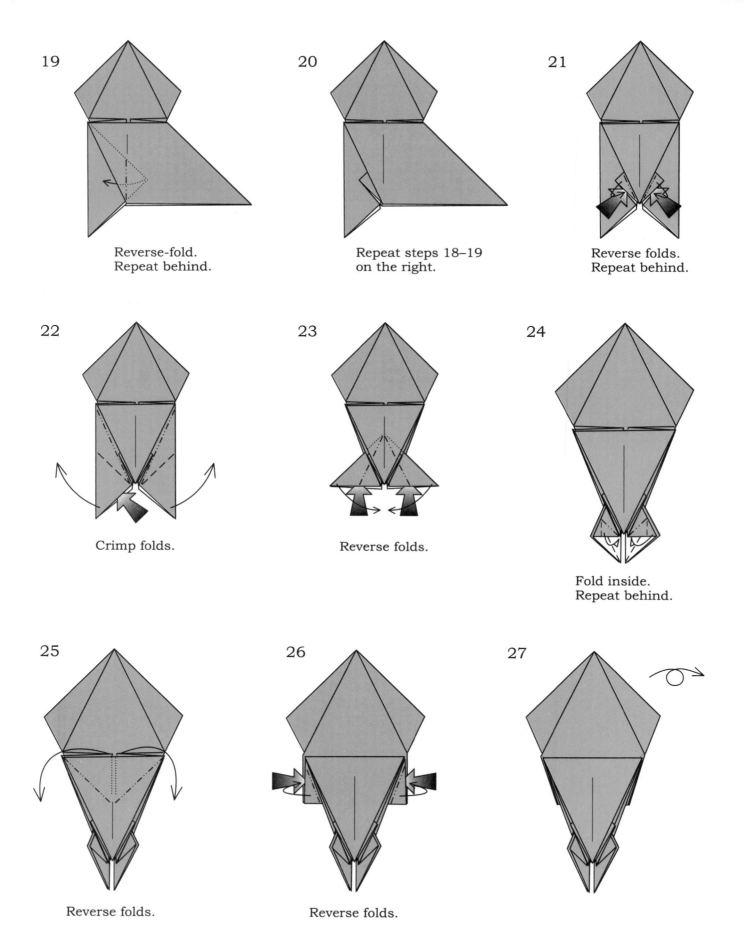

19

Reverse-fold.
Repeat behind.

20

Repeat steps 18–19
on the right.

21

Reverse folds.
Repeat behind.

22

Crimp folds.

23

Reverse folds.

24

Fold inside.
Repeat behind.

25

Reverse folds.

26

Reverse folds.

27

28

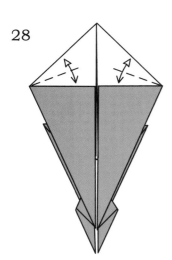

Fold and unfold.

29

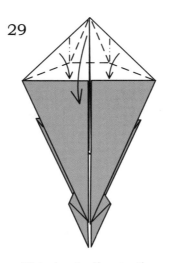

This is similar to the fold in the stretched bird base.

30

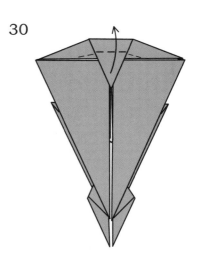

31

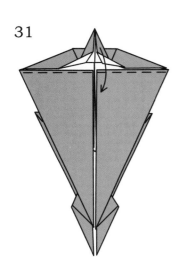

32

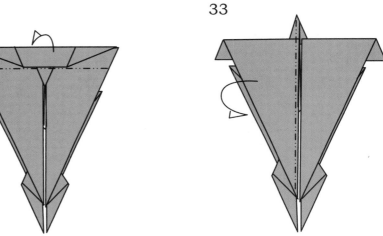

33

34

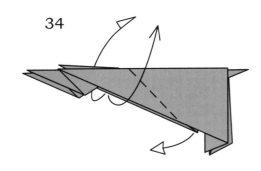

Outside-reverse-fold and swing the legs out.

35

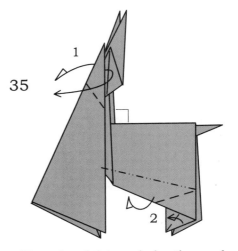

Note the right angle by the neck.
1. Outside-reverse-fold.
2. Fold the legs in half while thinning the body. Repeat behind.

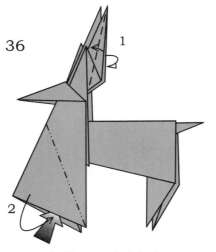

36

1. Repeat behind.
2. Reverse-fold.

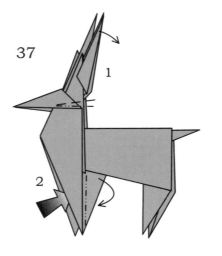

37

1. Crimp-fold.
2. Reverse-fold.

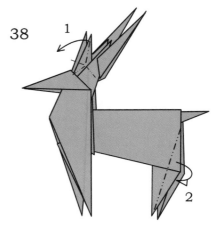

38

1. Double-rabbit-ear.
2. Tuck inside.
Repeat behind.

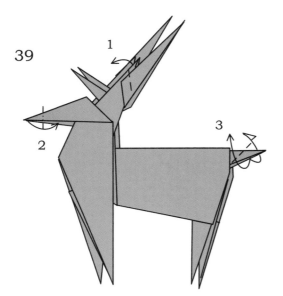

39

1. Fold only one horn down.
   Repeat behind.
2. Reverse-fold.
3. Outside-reverse-fold.

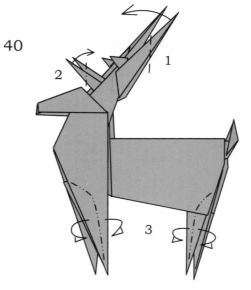

40

1. Outside-reverse-fold.
2. Reverse-fold.
3. Thin the legs.
Repeat behind.

41

Deer

Elephant

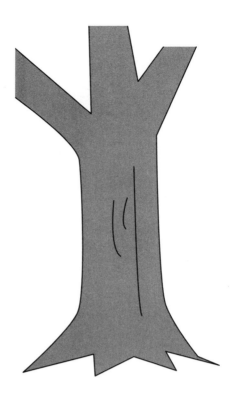

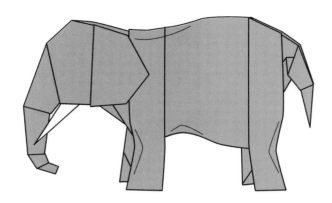

Elephants are fun to fold and fun to create. I have probably created more elephants than any other animal. This model is more challenging than other models in the book because it has white tusks.

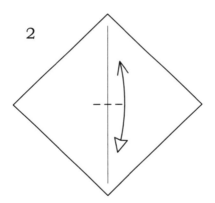

1

Fold and unfold.

2

Fold and unfold creasing in the center.

3

Fold and unfold creasing on the left.

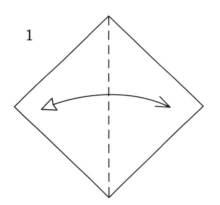

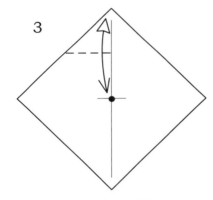

4

Fold the corner to the crease. Crease along the diagonal.

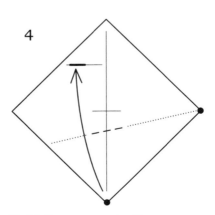

5

Unfold.

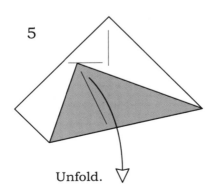

6

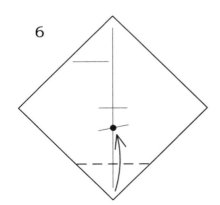

7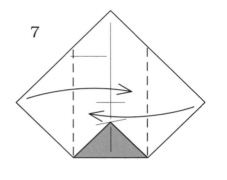

8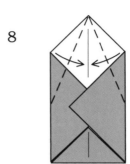

9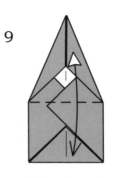

Fold and unfold.

10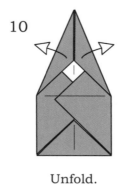

Unfold.

11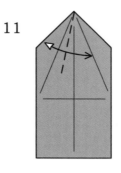

Fold and unfold.

12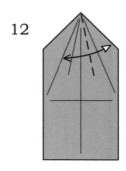

Fold and unfold.

13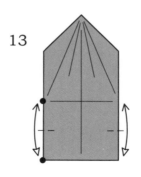

Fold and unfold
at the edges.

14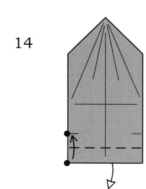

15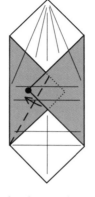

Mountain-fold
along the crease.

16

Unfold.

17

Fold the lower layer so
the edge meets the dot.

18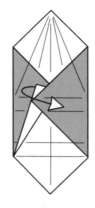

Unfold and bring the
layer to the front.

19

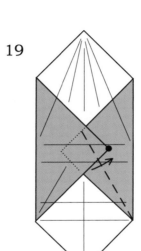

20

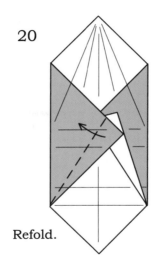

Refold.

21

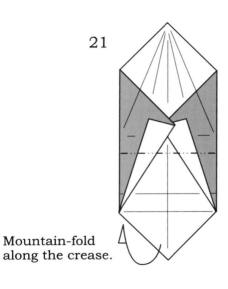

Mountain-fold along the crease.

22

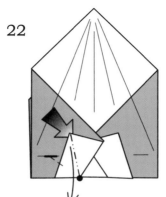

Begin with the mountain fold. Then fold on the valley line up to the horizontal crease.

23

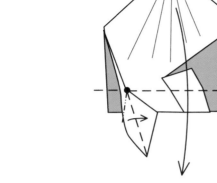

The model is 3D. Flatten.

24

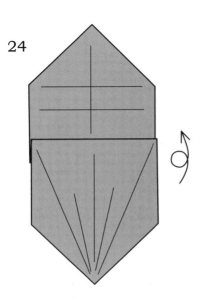

25

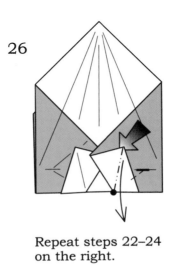

Unfold back to step 22.

26

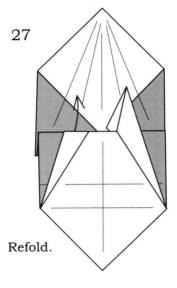

Repeat steps 22–24 on the right.

27

Refold.

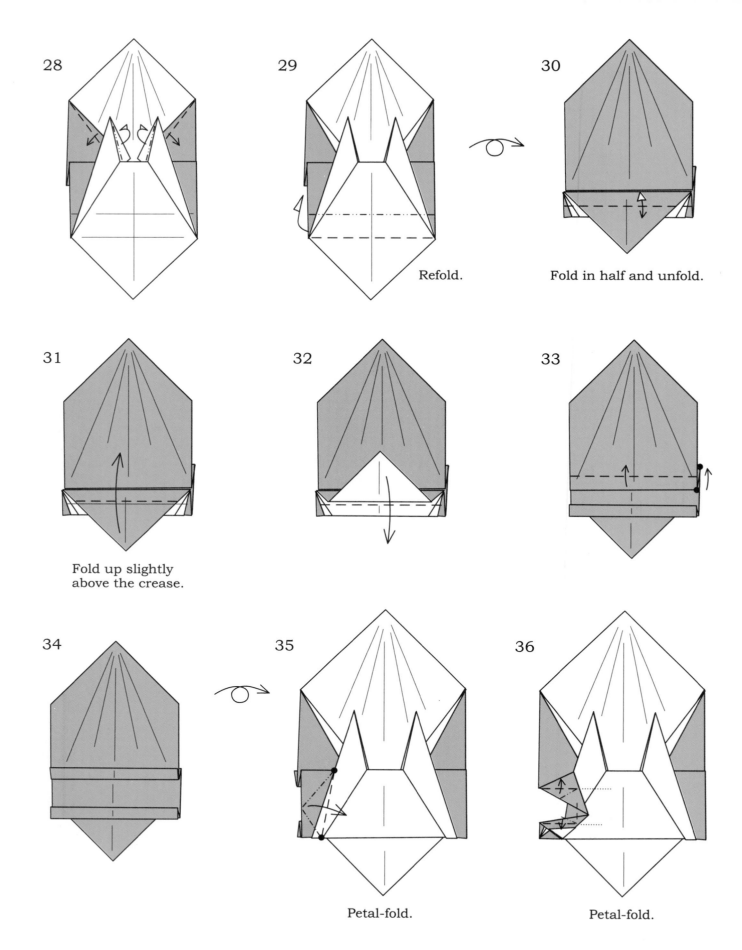

28

29

Refold.

30

Fold in half and unfold.

31

Fold up slightly
above the crease.

32

33

34

35

Petal-fold.

36

Petal-fold.

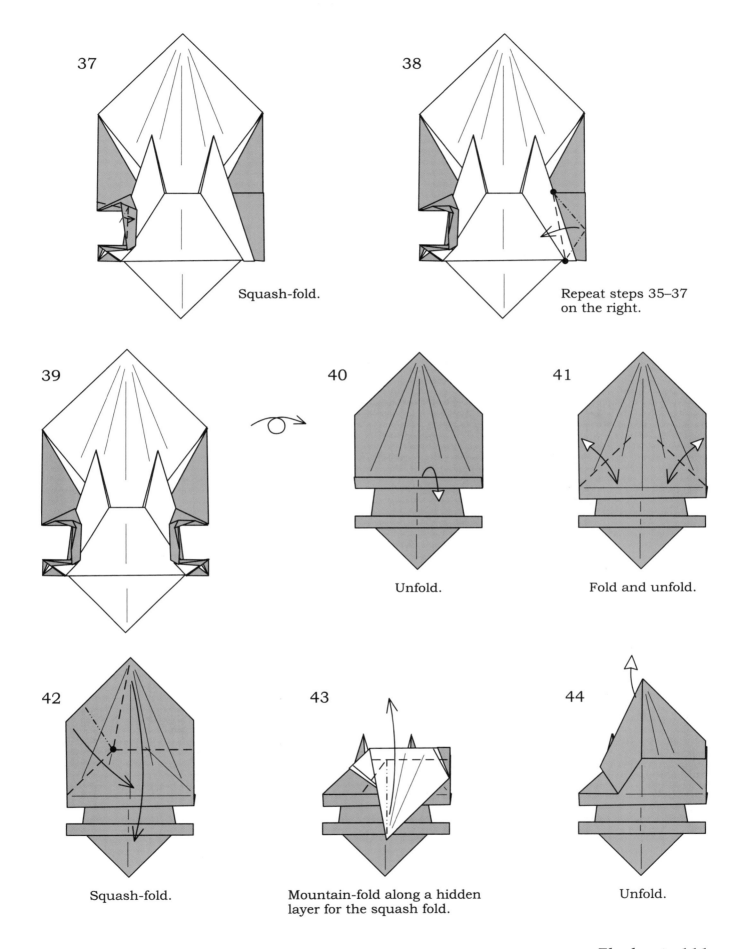

37

Squash-fold.

38

Repeat steps 35–37
on the right.

39

40

Unfold.

41

Fold and unfold.

42

Squash-fold.

43

Mountain-fold along a hidden
layer for the squash fold.

44

Unfold.

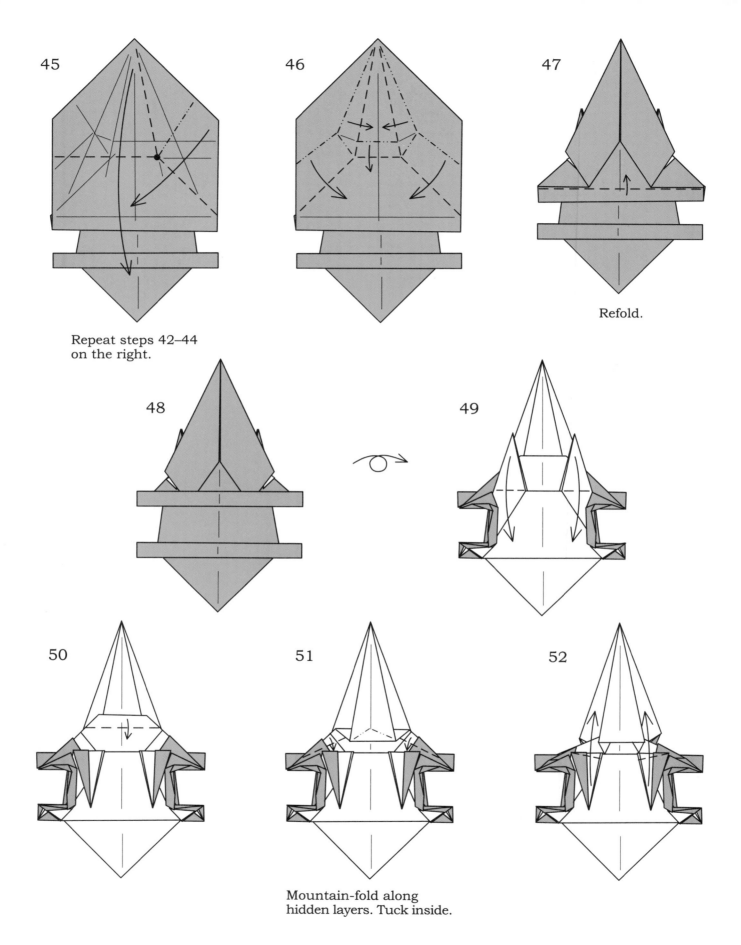

45

Repeat steps 42–44
on the right.

46

47

Refold.

48

49

50

51

52

Mountain-fold along
hidden layers. Tuck inside.

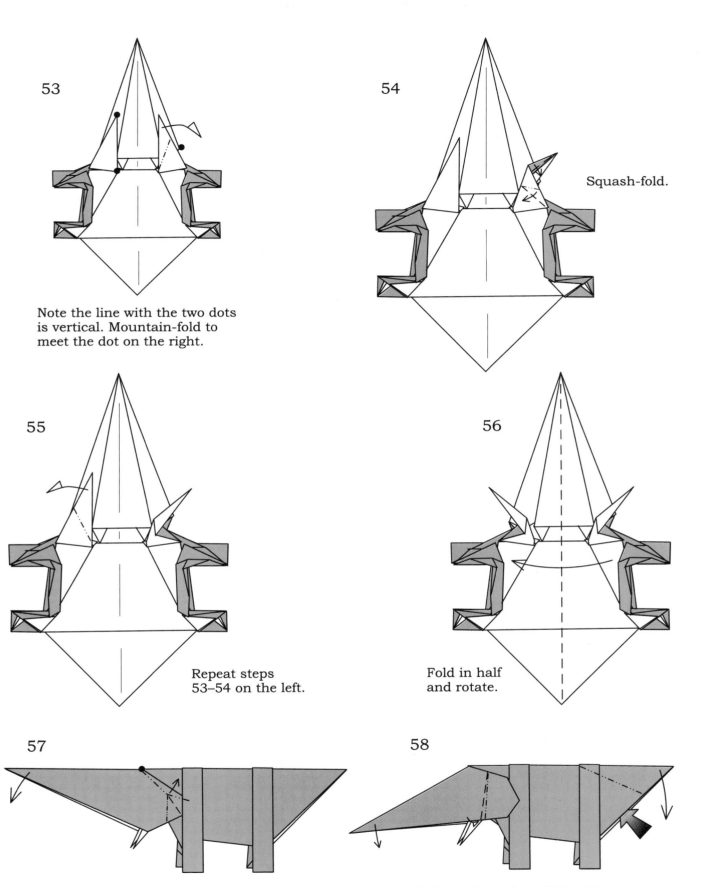

53

Note the line with the two dots is vertical. Mountain-fold to meet the dot on the right.

54

Squash-fold.

55

Repeat steps 53–54 on the left.

56

Fold in half and rotate.

57

Pivot about the dot to lift up at the ears and repeat behind.

58

Make a thin crimp-fold at the head. Reverse-fold at the tail.

59

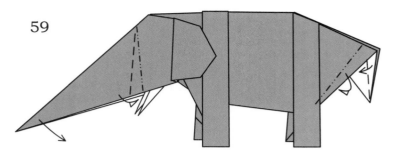

Crimp-fold the trunk. Trisect the angle at the tail and repeat behind.

60

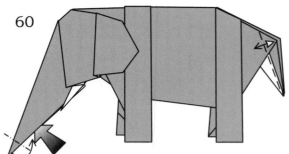

Reverse-fold at the trunk. Fold and unfold at the tail and repeat behind.

61

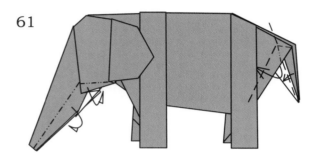

Repeat behind.

62

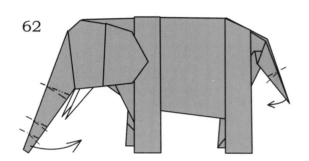

Crimp folds.

63

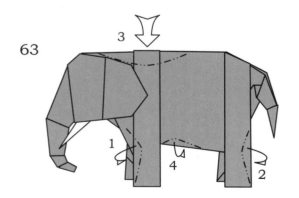

Curve the legs and body. Fold in order and repeat behind.

64

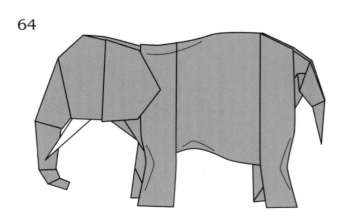

Elephant

Bee

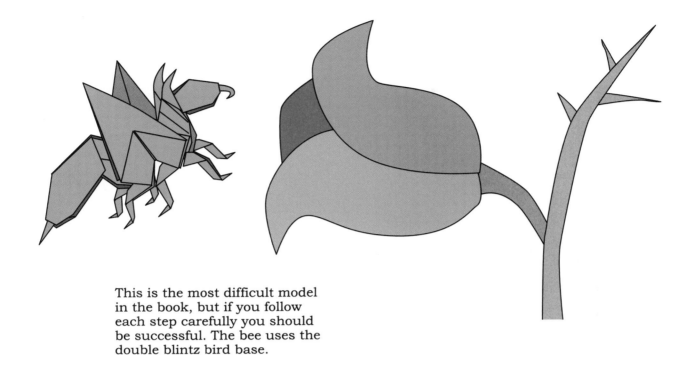

This is the most difficult model in the book, but if you follow each step carefully you should be successful. The bee uses the double blintz bird base.

1

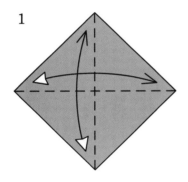

Fold and unfold.

2

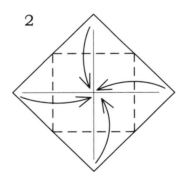

Blintz-fold.

3

Blintz again.

4

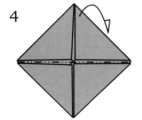

Fold in half.

5

Squash-fold.

6

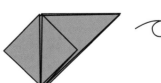

7

Squash-fold.

8

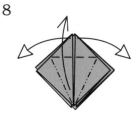

Petal-fold while pulling out the corners. Repeat behind. This is the same as steps 6–7 of the canary on page 70.

9

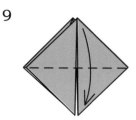

Repeat behind.

10

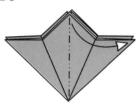

Spread the paper to unlock and pull out the flap.

11

Repeat step 10 on the back and sides.

12

Fold and unfold.

13

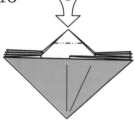

Sink.

14

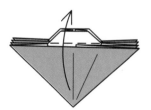

15

Repeat step 14 on the back and sides.

16

Note there is an inner flap in each of the four corners. Rotate.

17

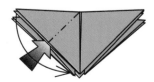

Squash-fold.

18

Repeat step 17 on the right and behind.

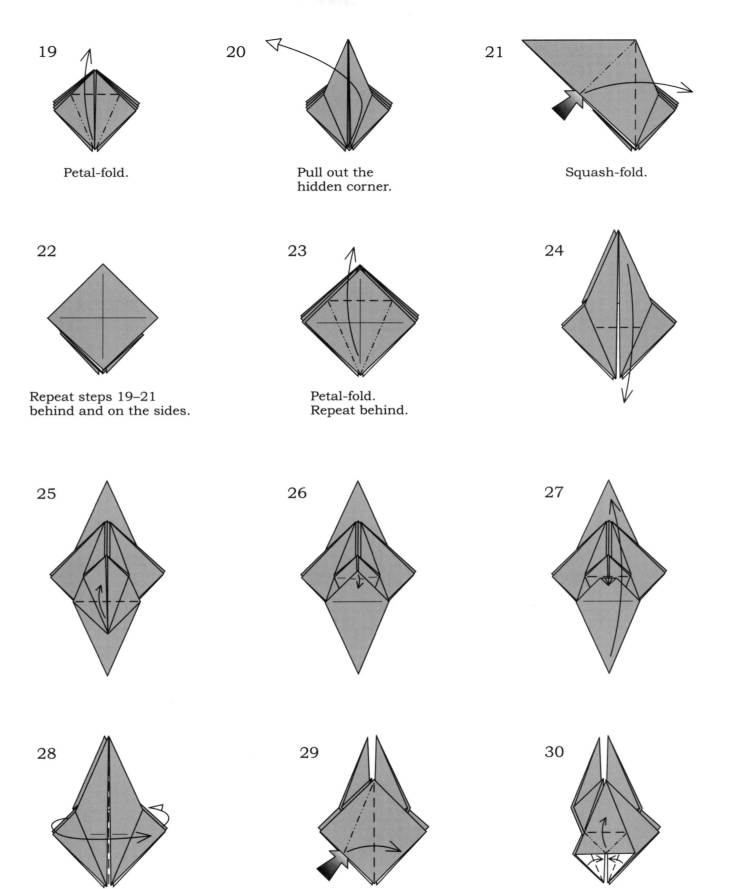

19

Petal-fold.

20

Pull out the
hidden corner.

21

Squash-fold.

22

Repeat steps 19–21
behind and on the sides.

23

Petal-fold.
Repeat behind.

24

25

26

27

28

Minor miracle.

29

Squash-fold.

30

Petal-fold.

31

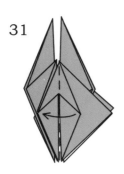

Repeat behind.

32

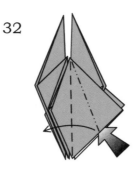

Squash-fold.
Repeat behind.

33

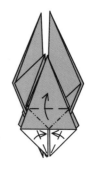

Petal-fold.
Repeat behind.

34

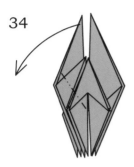

Reverse-fold.

35

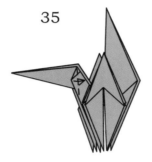

Repeat behind.

36

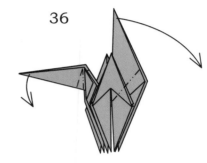

Crimp-fold at the head.
Reverse-fold the tail.

37

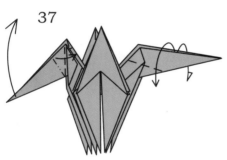

Crimp-fold at the head.
Outside-reverse-fold the tail.

38

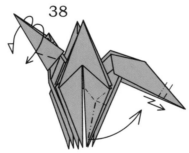

Outside-reverse-fold at the
head, crimp-fold the tail,
and double-rabbit-ear the
leg. Repeat behind.

39

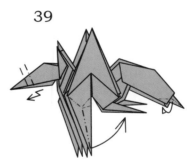

Repeat behind.

40

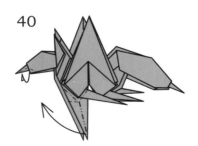

Repeat behind.

41

Repeat behind.

42

Bee

Basic Folds

Squash Fold

In a squash fold, some paper is opened and then made flat. The shaded arrow shows where to place your finger.

1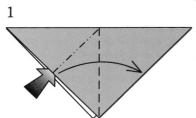

2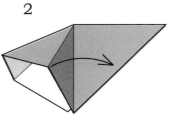

3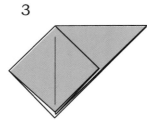

Squash-fold.   A 3D intermediate step.

Petal Fold

In a petal fold, one point is folded up while two opposite sides meet each other.

1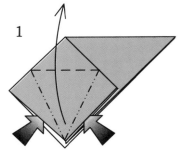

2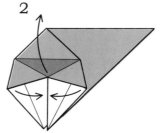

3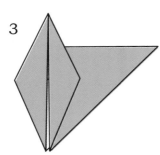

Petal-fold.   A 3D intermediate step.

Rabbit Ear

To fold a rabbit ear, one corner is folded in half and laid down to a side.

1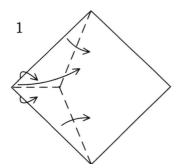

2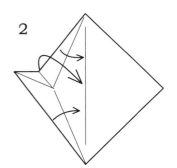

3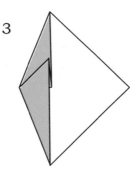

Fold a rabbit ear.   A 3D intermediate step.

Double Rabbit Ear

If you were to bend a straw you would be folding the double rabbit ear.

1 **2**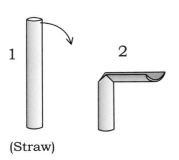

(Straw)

1 **2**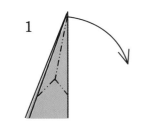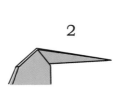

Make a double rabbit ear.

Inside Reverse Fold

In an inside reverse fold, some paper is folded between layers. Here are two examples.

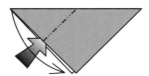

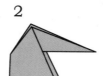

Reverse-fold.

Reverse-fold.

Outside Reverse Fold

For an outside reverse fold, the paper will wrap around itself. Much of the paper must be unfolded.

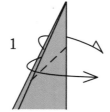

Outside-reverse-fold.

Crimp Fold

A crimp fold is a combination of two reverse folds.

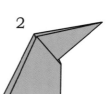

Crimp-fold.

Sink Fold

In a sink fold, some of the paper without edges is folded inside. To do this fold, much of the model must be unfolded.

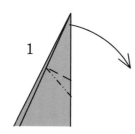

Sink.

Spread Squash Fold

A cross between a squash fold and sink fold, some paper in the center is spread apart and then made flat.

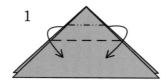

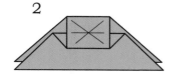

Spread-squash-fold.

120   *Teach Yourself Origami*